Donald Trump's Dominant Mind, Tragic Flaw, and Psychological Blind Spot

Peter Alan Olsson M.D.

Strategic Book Publishing
www.sbpra.com

For information about special discounts for bulk purchases, please contact Strategic Book Publishing at bookorder@sbpra.net.

ISBN: 978-1-63410-151-6

The only man who never makes a mistake is the man who never does anything.

Far better is it to dare mighty things, to win glorious triumphs, even though checkered by failure ... than to rank with those poor spirits who neither enjoy nor suffer much, because they live in a gray twilight that knows not victory nor defeat.

—Theodore Roosevelt

The Brothers Trump and Being a Winner ... Never, Ever a Loser!

Fred Trump Senior was so consumed with his business's success that he seemed to fuse his family's destiny with that of the Trump building and real estate company ventures. Fred Trump Senior had abnormally high expectations of success and **winning at all costs** for all his children and clearly for himself. He often used the expression "Be a killer" as an expression to spur on his children to be winners.

Donald Trump's brother, Fred Trump Junior, died in 1981 of a heart attack and alcoholism. Feeling the namesake focused pressure, Fred Trump Junior seemed to recoil against Trump Inc. and strongly proclaimed his individuating move toward his ambition to be an airline pilot. Fred Junior rejected a leadership position in the family business. Donald Trump chose, and was chosen, to join with his father in the company. Unfortunately, in the process, it appears that Fred Trump Jr. felt both pressure not to follow his bliss in flying but also a sense of rejection from his father in doing so. On one occasion, Fred Trump Sr. angrily put down Fred Jr.'s ambition to be an airline pilot as like being a bus driver in the sky. Donald, who was present, did not defend his brother on that occasion. Donald, subsequently, expressed admiration for his brother, and interestingly, he never drinks alcohol and as president supported alcohol treatment programs.

Donald Trump, a Battler

Donald J. Trump is easily disliked but frequently feared or respected by political opponents. He is difficult to love, and frequently misunderstood. President Trump is commonly maligned and devalued by many Americans. The anti-Trump phenomenon is notable among many psychiatrists, psychoanalysts, psychologists, and other mental health professionals. Many psychiatrists, psychologists, and psychoanalysts have written extensively about Trump's personality and psychology. Few of these writings, in my opinion, have been objective or even neutral toward Trump or his policies. Some have been openly derogatory and devaluing, such as the book *Deconstructing Trump: The Trump Phenomenon Through the Lens of Quotation History* (published September 23, 2019, by Dr. Mardy Grothe).

It is very important for me to clearly state that I have never examined Donald Trump or done a formal mental status examination. I have, however, observed Trump's political verbal and nonverbal behavior. I have read Trump's book and my psychiatrist and psychoanalyst colleagues' observations, opinions, and theories about Trump. I react critically toward my colleagues' opinions about Trump and often disagree.

One aspect of human nature is the strong tendency upon being insulted or devalued by another person, or observing a political leader doing such, is to cherry-pick a derogatory label for the insulter. Such quick labelling is often made preconsciously or unconsciously before systematic observations are accumulated and described. Early in his first campaign Donald Trump insulted Carly Fiorina's face, Marco Rubio's size, and Jeb Bush's energy level. The label narcissist, or malignant narcissist, for Trump began to be used by the press, laymen, and readily by psychiatrists and psychologists. Trump, like many presidents, is narcissistic.

President Trump has been devalued, even hated, and scorned for years by many in the liberal Democrat mainstream media (*The New York Times, The Washington Post*, CNN, MSNBC, NBC, CBS), the Washington establishment bureaucratic swamps, academia (particularly Ivy League political scientists and social scientists), and social media moguls at Facebook, Twitter, Google, and Amazon. Many pundits have labelled Trump's puffery, exaggerations, hyperbole, sarcastic humor, bragging, and ad hominem attacking political speechifying as destructive "lying." Major newspapers even kept running counts of Trump's supposed "lies." Trump loves his battle with the fake news media and academia. Trump's attacks and insults of opponents damage his message, yet Trump seems to embrace and enjoy the political combat. I have felt swept up in powerful ambivalent feelings about Trump and changed my mind about him more than once.

As a supporter of Donald Trump in 2000, I fully acknowledged his aggressive, negative traits, cruel ad hominem attacking of opponents, and extremely unorthodox political behavior and style. I also describe his **tragic flaw** and **psychological blind spot**. It led me to reassess my support for Trump after his behavior on January 6, 2021. I explain my reasons for questioning his leadership on January 6, 2021, later in this book.

Like all of us, Donald Trump has flaws, tragic flaws. **The tragic flaw of Donald Trump's personality is an obsession with winning at any and all costs.** His mantra is "never, ever, be a loser!" During Trump's maturation and psychological development, the relentless drive to succeed and **be a winner**, as his father demanded and rewarded, has dominated Donald Trump's life. It has led to deficits in Donald's capacity for empathy and nurturing of less aggressive and successful persons. Winning and working hard successfully gain Trump's respect and admiration. Trump's favored solutions for less fortunate people was primarily to provide jobs and work, hard work. Failures as a Trump employee meant, "You're fired." Even the initially beloved General "Mad Dog" Mattis suffered such fate from Trump, as did dedicated men like Rex Tillerson, Jeff Sessions, and William Barr.

A truth seems to elude Donald Trump: sometimes a loser who learns from the experience becomes a winner. Trump, a lover of sports, should have known that even if your team gets bad calls from the umpires, the other team cheats, and your team loses, you can learn from a defeat. Perhaps a comeback that Americans love will possibly happen for Trump in 2024.

Trump is by no means the only American president with obnoxious personality traits and obvious flaws. In a nation long divided politically before Trump was elected, I believe it is important to describe the authentic and positive core of Trump's motives, kept promises, and successful efforts to improve and help our country, often despite his abrasive personality and personal style.

In this book, I do not use an exclusively traditional applied psychoanalytic or psychobiographical approach toward understanding Donald Trump. I do make use of my knowledge and experience as a physician, psychiatrist, and psychoanalyst, but also make use of allegory, poetry, book review material, and literary essay format material in my approach.

My Initial View of Donald Trump

During the 2016 presidential campaign I was stunned, and often revolted, by Donald Trump's aggressive and insulting verbal behavior and political tactics. His comments about Carly Fiorina's face angered and disgusted me. At times, his ad hominem attacks on political opponents were beyond impolite. Such behaviors were harshly labeled as unpresidential by pundits.

As a psychiatrist and psychoanalyst, I took note of Trump's obvious narcissistic preoccupations and seeming relentless insecurity about criticism and demands for loyalty. His impulsive, punching, and counterpunching Tweets created social media chicken and egg dilemmas. Did Trump's political Tweet punches create the liberals' and liberal media's hatred of Trump and their incipient fake news attacks on Trump, or was Trump primarily asserting and righteously defending himself? In the long run both Trump and the mainstream media seemed to relish and profit from the combat. Trump and the liberal media have created and co-authored a modern American political reality TV world of P.T. Barnumesque proportions. Trump uses hyperbole and often outrageous dangerous sounding overstatement to dramatize his opinion or even proposed policy. In dialogue with North Korea's leader who he called "Little Rocket Man," Trump boasted of having bigger, more powerful rockets! This led to some playful and significantly positive dealings with Kim. Trump also used hyperbole and sarcasm stating that Putin was powerful as a leader and said it would not be bad if he, Trump, got along well with Putin. Trump has even inappropriately dramatized the need for all NATO nations to pay their fair share of defense spending by suggesting he might allow Putin to do as he pleased if they did not. It stirred President Biden's ire but got lots of attention to a valid issue for NATO. Trump's press conferences become like vivid episodes of a reality TV show. Ordinary buttoned-up, focus group prepared politicians seemed bland and colorless in comparison to Trump, the often outrageous bully and offensive political warrior. I frequently asked myself, if Trump did not aggressively defend himself and tout his accomplishments, who would (besides Fox News efforts to be fair and balanced)?

I also noted Trump's relentless and restless energy. My earliest observations about Trump were linked to Teddy Roosevelt. Trump seems to need little sleep and demonstrates unending energy, drive, and obsession with winning. Winning at all costs with no truck for losers by Trump! Is being "The Winner" Trump's strength here or tragic flaw? A good question! Unlike Teddy Roosevelt, who read many books a week, Trump seemed to pride himself in his minimalist reading program. This offends academics who enjoy mocking him about it. Trump learns by intuitive flurries of interactions and action words, not from words in books. For Trump, compassion, comforting, and empathy are mainly expressed in action, not words.

I Have Changed My Mind About Donald Trump Several Times

Over time, I became fascinated and increasingly impressed with Trump's successful campaign despite his blatantly unorthodox and bullying political tactics. In "modern" American politics, civility and politeness do not result in victory. Finding political dirt and untruthful mudslinging does; ask John McCain and Mitt Romney. Trump shunned "losers" like McCain and Romney. Trump would be a winner at any cost for America. Trump seemed to not give a damn about the smoldering resentments of "the losers" even if they likely came back to bite him politically, and they certainly did!

Psychoanalytic colleagues accuse Donald Trump of manifesting malignant narcissism, mental illness, cult leader status, and dangerousness! I do not agree with them.

It is important to note that narcissism is *not necessarily* a synonym for selfishness or destructive self-absorption. In normal personality development, self-love matures and develops through anxieties and challenges, just as the ability to love others also can grow and mature. Trump's obvious narcissism is a prominent thread within the complex skein of his remarkable ego strength and type A personality. A strong ego is not egotistical in the commonsense usage of the expression "big ego," but indicates in Trump accurate intuition, street-smart intelligence, and good judgment. Before anything else politically, Trump loves America first: its military, safety, sovereignty, and success.

Trump is strong enough to withstand the attacks of bitter Democrats who never thought Trump would win the presidency. Strong enough to take on "the swamp" of Washington politics, politically correct liberal university professor enemies, and a massively anti-Trump and a vicious liberal American press. As Trump said early in his first campaign, he knows personally where all the political bodies are buried in Washington and how the pay-to-play swamp games are negotiated and deals made. He promised to use his tainted insider experiences to drain the Washington political swamp, an almost impossible task.

Trump's Aggression and Hatred of Trump's Aggression

Why the intense hatred and despising of Donald Trump by significant sectors of the American large group self? Why psychologically does the "resist Trump at all costs" among many persons seem to go beyond the usual American political battling? Many conservative Trump supporters call the Democrats' vengeful bitterness toward Trump the **Trump Derangement Syndrome**. There is strong evidence for the validity of such a term.

Trump the Political Aggressor, Identification with Trump the Aggressor, and Hatred of Trump the Aggressor—by significant portions of the American Large Group Self * (*See appendix for **further** details about the large group self.)

In individual psychology, psychoanalysts describe **identification with the aggressor** in their work with individuals, particularly traumatized persons. There is a parallel process by which an individual's sense of himself as part of a group is formed. In essence, inner representations of ourself and ourself in a group are parallel and conjoined during early developmental and maturational experiences. As a result, **an American Large Group Self-Representation** is found in individual Americans as well as the existence of a **Collective American Large Group Self**. One way to understand a key domain of the American large group self or **will of the people** is the result of a presidential election. The American electorate is barraged with political campaign speeches, articles, presidential debates, political talking head "experts'" opinions about the debates, and the candidates. Candidates often write books about themselves, and favorable and unfavorable books about the candidates are abundant. The net result occurring at an election can, however, be viewed as a powerful expression of the unconscious will of the American large group self.

In observing Trump operate politically and the intense reactions to his flamboyant, hyperbolical, unorthodox, and aggressive style, I have been struck with what could be called psychological **identi-fication with or hatred of the aggressor**.

Love of Trump: Identification with Trump the Aggressor

In his large political rallies Trump is applauded, cheered, and adored by the crowds of supporters as he insults, demeans, and caricatures political opponents. They radiate an almost joyful identification with their aggressor hero. Many in Trump's campaign-style crowds have felt traumatized and hurt by trade and other government policies that they feel took their jobs away in the coal or manufacturing industries. Trump is, among other perceived political virtues, their aggressor savior. He extols winning and he is his supporter's winner for America to be forcefully made great again! Trump as a winner, makes America a winner again! Not a dreaded loser. Never!

Hate of Trump: Hatred of Trump the Aggressor

Democrats, and even some Republican politicians, resent and clearly hate Trump. This reflects, at a conscious or subconscious level, resentment of his aggressive bullying political behavior. For many Americans, haunted by puritanism or other reasons of self-esteem deficiency, we despise boastfulness. Many also seem to feel victimized or traumatized. Trump sometimes starts such political fights, and certainly, if attacked, will predictably escalate his aggression to win a personal fight to win at all costs. Many sectors of the American large group self react with a tone of narcissistic woundedness, rage, and seek political revenge at all costs. Trump despises losers, and Trump haters feel like he is calling them losers for not adoring him!

Nancy Pelosi, the Political Shrew that Couldn't Be Tamed by Donald Trump

A prototypical hater of Trump was/is Nancy Pelosi. From their earliest encounters as Speaker of the House and President, mutual hatred seemed assured. Trump blatantly called Nancy a terrible politician and neurotic. Pelosi denied hatred of Trump, saying as a good Catholic she prayed for Trump every day. Access to the content of Pelosi's prayers for Trump would be revealing. I wonder if C.S. Lewis's *The Screwtape Letters* would have found such prayers of great literary use.

Trump has been described by many people from all walks of life as charming and comfortable to be with, from professional golfers to Ronald Reagan, who is said to have remarked after a conversation, "After our talk, I felt like I had just talked to the president."

Trump not only did not charm Pelosi but he participated in an American political lover spat with her that massively impeded success in solving America's problems at many levels. Hell, hath no fury like two American political leaders participating in relentless mutual scorn.

Nancy Pelosi continues to join President Biden in blaming Trump for massive illegal immigrant problems at our southern US border, which have been triggered by Biden's undoing of Trump's successful policies on the border! In addition, Pelosi continues to create an ongoing myth that the capital needs a wall around it to protect against dangerous Trump followers without any clear evidence from US Intelligence.

The Press as the Attacker and the Attacked, "Fake News"

The biased and slanted liberal media typified by *The New York Times* is, in turn, attacked by Trump as "**fake news**." When verbally attacked we all tend to naturally react emotionally and defensively. Such is true of human nature as is to harbor conscious or unconscious levels of revenge-seeking. Trump's political enemies, and there are many of them, react like collective wounded political animals who will not accept Trump's election, nor will they support, compromise, and work with him politically or legislatively. Trump seems oblivious or in denial of the pain his ad hominem attacks on others inflict or the inevitable future retaliations that will occur. Trump's attacks of John McCain and Mitt Romney are prime examples. Romney seems to react like he is forced to take his awful tasting medicine when he agrees with Trump. McCain seemed, at one level, to relish scuttling Trumpcare with his thumbs down vote in the Senate.

Many sectors of the American large group self react with a tone of narcissistic woundedness, rage, and seek political revenge at all costs. One could argue that whole TV networks adore or despise Donald Trump. Their commentary and opinion staffs adore and defend Trump or lead and cheerlead the hate and despise Trump cadres. Political revenge-seeking and score-settling is rendering our representative democracy dysfunctional and Putin chuckles with glee. It is an interesting paradox that instead of Trump working with Putin to defeat Hillary, it was Trump's detractors of all stripes working with Putin to unwittingly hurt America.

Trump's Narcissism

Donald Trump, like many or most political leaders, is narcissistic. The reader should know, however, that narcissism is not a psychiatric curse word. The psychoanalytic term for the complex domain of self-love and dignity is narcissism, or the narcissistic sector of our personality. As I said earlier, narcissism is *not necessarily* a synonym for selfishness or self-absorption. In a normal personality, self-love matures and develops through anxieties and challenges, just as the ability to love others also can grow and mature. As the Bible clearly indicates, healthy self-love is necessary to love others.

Jesus replied: "Love the Lord your God with all your heart and with all your soul and with all your mind.' This is the first and greatest commandment. And the second is like it: 'Love your neighbor **as yourself**'" (Matthew 22:37-39, NIV).

It was Sigmund Freud who observed that we love *anaclitically* (relating to the mother who nurtured us, or the father who protected us) or *narcissistically* (relating to the self we wish we were, the self we used to be, or in affiliation with another self that reflects favorably upon us). Anaclitic literally means "leaning on," and refers to an infant's utter dependence on its mother or mother substitute for its sense of well-being and actual survival. Anaclitic love is pervasive normal behavior in early childhood, but not as much in adulthood. Trump seems in his adulthood to have developed a strong **reaction formation**[1] to any elements of a need for anaclitic love. Trump can very well protect and nurture himself, thank you very much; you citizenry of mothers, fathers, and children. Trump's sense of empathy and tenderness is guarded on the surface by toughness, aggression, and a strong will that can be misperceived as rigid stubbornness or coldness. Trump's love for America is expressed through winning elections and getting laws passed to support his policies. He told one audience, "You might get tired of winning, winning, winning!" Trump never loses, ever. For Trump, love of America is winning for America.

---

[1] **reaction formation:** A psychological defense mechanism, operating unconsciously, wherein attitudes and behavior are adopted that are the opposites of impulses the individual harbors either consciously or unconsciously (e.g., excessive moral zeal may be a reaction to strong but repressed asocial or antisocial impulses, or apparent willful stubbornness a strong accurate intuition the truth of which few people grasp).

Psychiatrists and Psychoanalysts Who Misperceive Trump

During my career of over fifty years in medicine, psychiatry, and psychoanalysis, I have observed that we psychodynamically oriented psychiatrists and certainly psychoanalyst psychiatrists, value words, "mentalizing" with words, and complex verbal interaction, insight, and emotional catharsis in the psychoanalytic process and conversation. This is, of course, a natural result of our training and experience. It is at the core of what and who we are in our professional identity.

However, some very effective and "normal" persons do not make use of psychotherapy methods or experiences in resolving their conflicts, maturing in their life, succeeding in their vocation, or relationships. Such effective persons are not any the less for their not participating in psychotherapy or psychoanalysis. Pros and cons can be argued as to whether a psychoanalysis would or would not benefit all American presidents. Ideally, a successful analysis would surely help a president and might very well lead a potential president to not consider pursuing the office.

Doing psychodrama therapy and supervising dance, music and art therapists have taught me about action therapies, cognitive behavior therapy applications, and other approaches to conflict resolution and maturation. Many successful people learn and grow through action, learning from failure and resilient trial and error learning. Donald Trump is such a person. He has navigated the rough and tumble failures and successes of the world of New York and other real estate dealings, "reality TV land" success, and the politics of *The Art of the Deal*. Trump's road in life bears little resemblance to many successful analysands and psychoanalysts. Trump is a man of action! Words for Trump are actions, because when he uses them, he means what he says and promises. He acts to keep his political promises and does not merely make speeches.

I think many psychiatrists, psychologists, and psychoanalysts would feel bowled over and intimidated at a non-doctor-patient interview by the aggressive, intuitive, and paradoxically charming Donald Trump. Or, for that matter, Lyndon Johnson in his political heyday. In fact, many psychiatrists seem to quickly mislabel Trump's actions and words as impulsive, impulse-ridden, lying, irrational, even dangerous. They seem to regard Trump's actions and words as technical "acting out"[2]as if he were in psychotherapy.

Acting out for many psychiatrists is thus tinged with a negative connotation. For some observers, acting out becomes synonymous with difficult, unruly, or destructive behavior, particularly in describing adolescents. Psychotherapist psychiatrists, psychologists, and psychoanalysts prefer their patients to use words to mentalize and reflect on a path to insight to resolve conflict and mature as persons in psychotherapy. Trump uses words as primarily actions and acts politically to back up and implement his words in executive action. Trump aggressively and relentlessly acts to keep his political promises. A kind of tough love form of empathy and compassion. Again, Trump's great strength or tragic flaw?

Justin Frank, MD, is only one of many psychiatrists and psychoanalysts who clearly regard Donald Trump as mentally ill, unstable, and probably dangerous to American's safety and collective American

---

[2] **acting out**: expression of unconscious emotional conflicts or feelings in actions rather than words. The person is not consciously aware of the meaning of such acts (American Psychiatric Association Glossary, 1994).

mental health. I disagree with my colleagues, and I think that many, like Dr. Frank, are swayed by their personal dislike of Trump to distort their analysis. To use a psychoanalytic concept, my colleagues react out of their transference or countertransference dislike, even hatred of Trump. Or they use the inner data of their countertransference feelings and fantasies to form biased theoretical formulations about Trump with flimsy secondhand supporting data from journalistic interviewers. They weaponize their theories about Trump to attack him in subtle or not very subtle ways. My book review thoughts below express my concerns about such politically weaponized psychoanalytic theory used against Donald Trump by Dr. Justin Frank.

Book Review Thoughts About Trump on the Couch: Inside the Mind of the President by Justin A. Frank, MD (2018), Published by Avery, an Imprint of Penguin Random House

In Justin Frank's book about Donald Trump, he brilliantly describes the psychoanalytic theorizing of Melanie Klein in ways an educated layman can understand. However, Kleinian language tends to project and portray human thoughts, feelings, and fantasies in stark monolithic ways. Ordinary mother-infant interactions are cast in terms of good breasts, bad breasts, good mother, and bad or frustrating mother labels. Klein at times portrays the mother-child interactions as if the mental apparatus of an infant and young child has developed and retained precise perceptions far beyond the actual cognitive and mentalization abilities of a child's actual age-related Piagetian developmental phase of development.

Frank gives cogent and perceptive descriptions of the dynamics of racism, the psychology of misogyny, lying, and the psychological implications of persisting dyslexia, and reading and learning disability in adults. It is when Frank applies such concepts to Donald Trump that his countertransference of anxiety, fear, and dislike of Trump peek pointedly through his observations and theorizing.

Frank uses anti-Trump polemical writers and biographers of Trump as sources of "data" for his speculative, conjecturing, and at times, condescending, even theoretical, rhapsodizing about Trump's psychopathology. For example, after biased speculations about Trump's "birther" concerns about President Obama, Frank says this on page 97:

> While Donny was a legitimate child, he was not necessarily one, because he already had an older brother named for their father. No matter how much his father loved him, Donny ["Donny"? Really, Doctor Frank? Seems snarky in tone by Frank] would never be Fred Trump, Jr.—his father's legitimate namesake.

Does namesake so sweepingly determine legitimacy and destiny? Frank uses such predicate or paleo-logic often about Trump in his book. Parenthetically, I could speculate differently from Frank that Trump was correct about Obama's birth. Psychologically and psychodynamically speaking, Obama seems to have been born an Indonesian candidate, not Hawaiian American, whatever his birth certificate indicated.

Frank describes an emotional rant by Trump on a *Fox & Friends* TV show on pages 232-233. Frank calls Trump's angry ventilating about James Comey, FBI, CNN, and Robert Mueller, a "continued paranoid portrayal of himself as victim."

My view is, as valid as Frank's psychoanalytic sanctimony is about Trump, Trump was appropriately angry about strong emerging evidence that James Comey, Comey's lead investigator Peter Stzrok, and acting FBI director Andrew McCabe were like Mueller's legal team, at best heavily biased against Trump, and likely seeking to discredit Trump and destroy him politically. Would Frank want Trump to repress his appropriate ire? Or express his feelings and thoughts with unvarnished directness on the one American TV network (FOX) that is not biased against him at every turn. The liberal elite American media and academia have viciously personally attacked, without basis, Trump's wife, his young son, and his loyal, effective adult children. Such never occurred with media-adored president Obama and his family.

Frank says toward the end of his book, "The goal of this study has never been to diagnose but to observe, comprehend and provide some context, to improve our understanding of the characteristics of Trump's behavior." In my opinion, Frank is rationalizing and deceiving himself and perhaps his reader. It would be more honest if Frank stated openly that his book is an applied clinical psychoanalytic polemical study that is biased and anti-Trump. Frank attempts to sound scientific, objective, and clinical, but he uses psychoanalytic concepts as political cudgels against Trump.

Frank weaponizes linguistic analysis, psychoanalytic theory, and psychiatric concepts. Between, and in his lines, Frank portrays Trump as an ultimately dangerous, untreatable, malignant narcissist, and psychopathic paranoid, pre-psychotic, with lifelong dyslexia, paramnesia, and learning/reading disabilities!

In his psychoanalytically weaponized anti-Trump book, *Trump on the Couch*, psychoanalyst Justin Frank describes Donald Trump and his preadolescent chum Peter Brant's challenges to authority. Donald and Peter liked to sneak on the subway from Queens to Manhattan on Saturdays. They delighted in going to a magic shop at West 49th Street and Broadway where they bought stink bombs, smoke bombs, plastic fake vomit, and hot pepper gum they gave to unsuspecting classmates. Exciting scenes in *Westside Story* drew their fascination to switchblade knives, which they secretly collected. Frank notes these forays by Trump and his buddy, Peter, as a key reason that Trump's father placed him in the New York Military Academy after seventh grade. Also, a factor involved in Fred Trump's decision to send

Donald to military school was Donald's bad behavior and academic reports from the school at which his he was a trustee. Fred Trump was a proud man very aware of his image and reputation.

Frank implies this was a traumatic banishing of Donald from the family home and an exile to military school. Another reasonable and the correct interpretation is that Donald Trump needed more structure and supervision than his father could provide. Fred Trump sensed unconsciously or consciously what Donald needed at that point in his life was more structure, which a military school provided. Fred Trump was strong and empathic enough to make the decision to send Donald to the increased social structure and presence of authority at military school. It is interesting that to this day, Trump's respect for, valuing, and idealization, of the US Military is prominent.

Donald's military school experience can also be Donald Trump's early assertion of necessary independence and pushing away from parents whose own neurotic personality problems and limitations needed to be transcended and compensated for in new ways. Donald's older brother, Fred Trump Jr., eventually wilted under the burden of his father's expectations of high financial achievement and relentless expectation of being a winner. Donald Trump does not wilt under pressure and enjoys the fray of the blood sport of American political battles.

More About Politically Weaponized Psychoanalytic Theory Used Against Donald Trump

As a Trump supporter among American psychoanalysts, I think Trump to be effectively psychologically compensated in some unusual ways. He has transcended his alleged dyslexia, reading/learning disability, and neurotic character disorders of his parents to wield political power in unusual, often unorthodox, ways in the Washington swamp.

Other Psychiatrist and Psychoanalyst Attackers of Donald Trump
In Psychodynamic Psychiatry, 46(3) 335–356, 2018, of The American Academy of Psychodynamic Psychiatry and Psychoanalysis Larry S. Sandberg, M.D., Clinical Associate Professor of Psychiatry at Weill Cornell Medical College; Lecturer, Columbia University Center for Psychoanalytic Training and Research conducted **an extensive interview with Dr. Bandy Lee a forensic psychiatric expert on violence.**

Dr. Lee opines extensively how, in her opinion, mentally disturbed, disturbing, and dangerous President Donald Trump is for America. According to the New York Times, *The Dangerous Case of Donald Trump* is a 2017 book edited by Bandy X. Lee, a forensic psychiatrist, containing essays from psychiatrists, psychologists, and other mental health professionals describing the "clear and present danger" that US President Donald Trump's mental health poses to the nation and individual well-being of Americans and, by implication, the world.

In an article in *Psychodynamic Psychiatry* (Vol 47 #2, Summer 2019, pp 149-165) "Some Comments on the Alternative Universe of the Trump Administration" by Graeme J. Taylor, MD, **A Critical Opinion Discussion by Peter A. Olsson, MD**, I expressed firm disagreement with politically weaponized use of psychoanalytic theory and psychiatry against Donald Trump by Dr. Taylor, Dr. Lee, Dr. Lifton, and many other colleagues, saying:

> In regard to our American President Donald Trump, Dr. Graeme Taylor (a distinguished Canadian psychiatrist and psychoanalyst) and I have starkly different opinions [about President Trump]. We have a "Causality Dilemma." In essence, has President Trump and his personality, phallic aggression, and hugely unorthodox political behavior caused the hatreds, divisions, fears,

anxieties, and deep-seated political differences in America and beyond? Or is Trump looked to as a charismatic, aggressive leader at a crucial time in history to radically rebuild an American national image of economic and military strength; and reform the gridlock and "swamp" of corruption and ineffective leadership in Washington DC? After eight years of what many Americans think was tepid leadership by Barack Obama as commander-in-chief, the need for returning America to a strong, diplomatic leadership position in the world backed by military strength was long overdue.

Trump Derangement Syndrome

Many psychologists and psychiatrists state or imply that Trump is mentally ill, endangers America, and damages mental health in America and beyond. I stoutly disagree with these colleagues and think they basically dislike Donald Trump as a person. Their negative countertransference feelings toward Trump lead to negative projections on to Trump. The projections often take the form of "Wild Applied Psychoanalysis"[3] and **psychologically weaponized theorizing**.

For example, Dr. Taylor referred in his article to the intriguing and fascinating formulations of noted French psychoanalyst Janine Chassequet-Smirgel, about the theoretical underlying psychodynamics behind sexual perversions and extremist ideologies. Dr. Taylor misused Chassequet-Smirgel's notion of an "anal universe" or "alternate universe" to abstractly and theoretically frame alleged distortions in Trump and his follower's cognition, and even erroneously posits that a Trump-based perversion of the truth is leading

---

[3] **Wild Psychoanalysis:** A term introduced in 1910 by Sigmund Freud (1856–1939) in an article entitled "'Wild' Psycho-Analysis" (Standard Edition, XI, pp. 221–7).

to absence of moral constraints, ethical principles, and pleasurable sadomasochistic fantasies involving dominance and power over America and in America!

Dr. Taylor also mentioned Dr. Bandy Lee's allegation in an interview in an earlier issue of *Psychodynamic Psychiatry* that the pattern of Trump's alleged lying is "at least partially delusional"! I think Trump merely used political puffery, hyperbole, or campaign sarcasm. Taylor also described Robert J. Lifton's concept of "malignant normality" by which Lifton attacks Trump. (Lifton's essay appeared in Dr. Lee's 2017 book). Lifton apparently thinks Trump threatens the viability of American democracy! I said in my critique that America's constitutional democratic republic is not as fragile as Lifton implied. I urged Dr. Lifton to recall the hard, staccato body count data of Robert McNamara and LBJ's delusions of grandeur as President Johnson escalated the horrors of our lost war in Vietnam. How would Lifton regard Obama's snide attacks and devaluations of the Fox News Network? Our American democratic republic's viability survived LBJ and Nixon as it will surely survive American's hatred or idealization and adoration of Trump and his bombastic, superlative-laced, and highly unorthodox intuition-based political style.

Dr. Taylor proceeded to cull out from anti-Trump journalistic writings a series of Trump's campaign-style comments or taken out-of-context statements to use as pseudoanalytic data to support group psychological formulations about Trump's alleged group psychological transgressions against persons with physical disabilities, women, journalists, and immigrants. Taylor neglected media data about Trump's efforts to clarify or successfully defend against such accusations by journalists. Unlike gentlemen like George W. Bush, John McCain, and Mitt Romney, Trump fights back rigorously.

Taylor discussed the separation of immigrant children from parents at our American crisis-scourged, southern border as psychoanalytic data against Trump. Taylor neglected to mention the fact that the child separation policy started with President Obama, and the fact that the whole overwhelming immigration nightmare was caused by many decades of neglect of the issue by the American Congress and several presidential administrations with politically timid heads in the sand. Trump supporters could reply that Trump at least tries to confront and resolve the political large group issues even if with blunt ineffective political instruments at times. The economic, social, cultural, and medical facts are that the US simply cannot handle hundreds of thousands and even millions of illegal immigrants massing and turning themselves in at our border to then disappear into shadowlands in our country never to appear at their asylum hearings.

In a final section, Taylor presents intriguing ideas about rampant phallic symbolism and chauvinistic, misogynistic themes in Trump's speechifying, psychoanalytic theory, and the psychohistory of American politics. Traditional maleness and femaleness like narcissism are not necessarily toxic psychologically, but as Carl Jung described with his discussion of the integration of the anima and animus, individuation and maturation for men and women is possible, even for American politicians and voters. As a biased supporter of Trump, I observed how positively Trump has been aided and helped by the impact of his daughter and his wife as well as his female staff and colleagues in his cabinet. Trump's engaged and positive ninety minutes with the remarkable Queen of England and straightforwardness in discussions with female world leaders can be seen as nontoxic masculinity.

J. L. Moreno, MD, regarded as the father originator of psychodrama, used to define clinically applied creativity in psychodrama as searching for new wisdom in action in the present clinical situation, or the use of old wisdom applied in new ways. In that sense, it can be asked if Trump's creative phallic aggression and *Art of the Deal* dynamic speechifying metaphors are not necessarily toxic for America after eight years of Obama's passive leadership and political drifting toward socialistic political ideas and theories.

An Alternative View of Donald Trump and His "Alternative Universe"

American voters usually are exposed to a variety of clever political demagoguery, obfuscations, deceptions, and a spectrum of lies, from little white ones to whoppers. Americans have had exposure to myriad forms of political lying over many presidential administrations. With Donald Trump's bombastic style, a new glossary of terms is needed to understand his evolving policies and predict his way of campaigning, leading, and governing. The new glossary would include words and concepts such as bombast, puffery, sarcasm (often cruel), strategic exaggeration, overt insults, crude personal verbal attack, hyperbolic impulsive statements to focus large group attention, paradoxical intention, mixed simultaneous use of an object as symbol and reality. (I.e., an actual wall, a wall as the need for clear national boundaries and rules of behavior and the inner psychological mindfulness and boundaries that comes with rugged, elemental, ego strength). And finally, many Americans admire Trump's extemporaneous, spontaneous free associations about the powerful emotions beneath political issues, ambivalent political relationships, and evolving policy statements. To my observation, many American voters find it refreshing and admirable that Trump answers questions without the focus group derived and calculated political speak of politically correct answers. He shares his thinking and feelings as much as national security allows. Trump defies academic ivory tower applied psychoanalytic approaches and projections of psychoanalytic theory at him and his effort to improve Americans' lives. Study of Trump's bestseller *The Art of the Deal*, business applications of Chaos Theory, and Saul Alinsky's Rules for Radicals are perhaps better tools to understand Trump's political behavior than psychoanalytic textbooks.

In conclusion about psychoanalytic writing about politics and politicians, I said in my opinion article:

> (1) In the domain of applied psychoanalysis and especially in describing politicians it is easy to slip over the line into using psychoanalytic theory as a psychological polemical cudgel rather than an objective analytic tool. Genuine neutrality and objectivity are hard to muster upon entering the psychoanalytic study of politics.

> (2) Our American president is not our country's psychiatrist, large group therapist, social worker, or pastor. He is primarily our chief executive, national and international leader and policy maker, commander-in-chief, signer, and chief enforcer of our laws, who makes important appointments. We psychoanalysts, as citizens, are free to express our thoughts and opinions about our president, his leadership style, his personality, and consequences of his words and policies. But, because of our professional training, clinical experience, status, or lack of it in American society, we need to take care to make every effort to not politically weaponize our theories, observations, and opinions in the endlessly important, but ambivalent, emotionally charged, and consequential domain of politics. Medical colleagues, general psychiatrists, and the informed public, rely on our clear, objective, reasonable use, and explication of our applied psychoanalytic theories.

The Media as Negative Messenger in the American Group Self—"Fake News"

Many sectors of the American large group self react with a tone of narcissistic woundedness, rage, and seek political revenge towards Trump at all costs. One could argue that whole TV networks adore or despise Donald Trump. Their commentary and opinion staffs adore and defend Trump or lead and cheerlead the hate of Trump. *The New York Times, The Washington Post,* and CNN are flagrantly, dishonestly, and destructively biased against Trump! Trump relishes the combat with "Fake News."

For Donald Trump in this sense, aggression and narcissism, in themselves, are neither "good" nor "bad" psychologically. An appropriate amount of narcissism is necessary for healthy self-esteem, good sense of humor, empathy, and creative expression. Trump's unique Art of the Deal political and governing style is blunt and crude, but a creative leadership instrument. Aggression and winning at any cost are the imperative for Trump. He must never ever be the loser! The liberal media seems obsessed with declaring or trying to make Trump a loser.

Trump has made plenty of mistakes in life and loving, but despite significant arrogance and self-centeredness has had victories as well. He finally found a remarkable, talented, and strong woman, Melania, to love and be loved. His children are attractive, talented, loyal, admiring, and devoted to Donald Trump. Trump seemed to grow in energy, political strength, and resolve as his time in office passed. Even crude and revolting attacks on his wife and family have not dented Trump, his marriage, or his family. A massively anti-Trump liberal American press campaign against Trump seems as endless as it is unsuccessful.

The New York Times relentless distorting, slanting of facts, misunderstanding and underestimation of Trump are stunning. *The New York Times* reporters should read Trump's book, *The Art of the Deal,* carefully. For example, when Trump comments about destroying sacred Iranian cultural sites, if necessary, in a possible war with Iran, it is a typical first step in his blatantly unorthodox style of conducting foreign policy and trade negotiations. Trump first gets an opponent's emotional attention! Trump then, like with "Little Rocket Man's" little rockets, compared to Trump's bigger ones, proceeds with the give and take of negotiations with Kim Jong Un of North Korea.

Trump is constantly misunderstood and underestimated by the liberal media, liberal academics, and the massive US state department and other bureaucracies. Trump's foreign, economic, or war policies are not didactic, traditional academic productions and lists, but fluid, flexible negotiated deals. The art of making deals to win. Always, WIN.

Trump, Obama, and Celebrity Power in the American Presidency

Barack Obama's personality was and is enormously different from Donald Trump's (*The Trojan Horse President: Observations and Opinions About Barack Obama's Leadership, Personality and Politics,* by Laurence Messner and Peter Olsson (2019) SBPRA, Houston). Was this contrast a key factor in Trump being elected? Perhaps. But Trump's personality and politics have as many complexities as does Barack Obama's. For example, Trump's so-called "lies" are often puffery and self-promoting reality TV self-dramatizations not completely unlike Obama's romanticized self-creating idyllic narratives in his famous book, *Dreams from My Father*! Trump's creative, lively Tweeting is an artform like Obama's eloquent speechifying behavior. These two creative, political, self-promoting, political, celebrity personalities are in a sense remarkable TV productions in themselves. Their two personalities and leadership styles can be seen as a strange yin and yang[4]: Obama's yin causing Trump's yang to be elected; yet Trump's yang causes a deep nostalgia for Obama's yin by Obamaites

---

[4] In Chinese philosophy, **yin and yang** is a concept of dualism in ancient Chinese philosophy, describing how seemingly opposite or contrary forces may actually be complementary, interconnected, and interdependent in the natural world, and how they may give rise to each other as they interrelate to one another. Two principles, one negative, dark, and feminine (*yin*), and one positive, bright, and masculine (*yang*), whose interaction influences the destinies of creatures and things (Wikipedia).

who despise Trump.

In addition, and in essence, the ever burgeoning and powerful celebrity status of presidents and ex-presidents is important to discuss before proceeding further with this psychological study of Donald Trump.

Celebrity Power and the US Presidency

Over recent decades American presidents have increasingly become TV celebrities. After they serve, they continue to gain notoriety, fame, and often great wealth. Such celebrity status affords them opportunities to do good things or to become or appear to be self-promoting and corrupt. Celebrity power is the domain of individual and group narcissism that allows the elevation of the social status of one individual above others because of his or her power, prestige, fame, and public adoration. Such celebrity power is co-authored. The gratification of the celebrity's narcissism is sustained in his glorified or envied status by the needs of the large group or society for heroes, entertainers, villains, or seers.

Trust, Charm, Charisma and Sincerity.

What is it about the importance of **charm**, **charisma**, and particularly, projected **sincerity** for would-be president celebrities to be successful? Celebrity presidents are also helped by a hint of "Bad-Boyishness" or "Bad-Girlishness" to enhance the individual's charm and charisma. If these traits go too far into fast-talking glibness, sincerity fades into lack of public trust. Richard Nixon, LBJ Vietnam rants, Bill and Hillary Clinton, and Barack Obama's speeches hover on the borderline between trust and the purgatory of arrogant prevarication and obfuscation.

Comebacks

Americans also admire comebacks among our celebrity presidents. Jimmy Carter had major economic and foreign policy failures during his presidency. However, Carter had a comeback as an ex-president. He has been successful as a philanthropist, author, and would-be international peacemaker. Richard Nixon mounted more than one comeback. After his resigning the presidency in disgrace, he became an author and sought-after pundit. Bill Clinton successfully assembled an amazing comeback in New Hampshire, despite his impeachment and tawdry affair with White House intern Monica Lewinsky, who was the age of Clinton's daughter. Clinton had lied directly to the American people while attempting sincerity. Recent questions about the ethics and legalities of his Clinton Foundation have not yet totally diminished the affection many Americans still feel towards Clinton. He is commonly seen as a redeemed ex-president doing good philanthropic work and getting high fees for speeches.

The Magic Charm of Words for US Celebrity Presidents
Speechifying is obviously of vital importance for celebrity presidents. Even as far back as FDR's "Fireside Chats," media prayer meetings with the American people, and his inspiring wartime speeches, we can see the early power of presidential celebrity-ism. Speech acquisition is a decisive step in the foundation of the executive domain of the human mind. In this sense, a child's earliest speech is a magic charm. It is directed toward forcing the external world and fate to do those things that have been conjured up in words. It is a serious question as to whether Barack Obama has, in some areas, had an adult reality check. The adoring US media has been loathed to examine Obama's new emperor's garb. Obama even was awarded the Nobel Peace Prize for accomplishments apparently anticipated but nonexistent at the time it was awarded, and to this day is of questionable validity.

Obama's Charm, Charisma, and Celebrity Status.
Barack Obama's smile and boyish charm helped him survive a difficult childhood. His charm also helped create and sustain his daz-

zlingly rapid ascendance to political power. David Maraniss, in his book about Obama, describes Barack's comment in an English class at Punahou school as they discussed **what people fear the most**. Obama said:

> WORDS …words are the power to be feared most … whether directed personally or internationally, words can be weapons of destruction.

As one observes Obama's verbal skills in action, it is impressive how he entwines graceful movements, a winsome smile, and a smooth charm to accompany his powerful wielding of words. His verbal-based charisma is connected to the timing of his rising and falling baritone intonations. Barack Obama, however, seems spellbound by the fantasy of the imagined pure power of his words, "as if" the programs and policies he talks about, and their successful results, were already on record. As an ex-president, it was predictable that Barack Obama would be an ever-rising celebrity star of progressive, left-wing Democrat causes. Obama lies, deceives, and obfuscates with an amazingly cool, though spurious, political effectiveness. Perhaps too cool to be true. Obama is a passive professorial aggressor. Trump uses words as political actions in different but equally powerful but AGGRESSIVE-AGGRESSIVE ways.

Donald Trump's Celebrity-ism

Donald Trump was an established celebrity and media star gatherer of his apprentices before deciding to run for president. His celebrity star was a tarnished one for years prior to his campaign. American voters are usually exposed to a variety of clever political demagoguery, obfuscations, deceptions, and a spectrum of lies, from little white ones to whoppers. As I often say, with Donald Trump's bombastic campaign style, **a new glossary of terms** is needed to understand his evolving policies and predict his way of leading and governing. The new glossary would include words and concepts such as bombast, puffery, braggadocio, sarcasm (cruel at times), overt insults, crude personal verbal attack, hyperbolic impulsive statements to focus large group attention, paradoxical intention, mixed simultaneous use of an object as symbol and reality (i.e., an actual wall, a wall as needed for clear national boundaries and rules of behavior), and extemporaneous Tweeted free associations about the powerful emotions beneath political issues, ambivalent political relationships, and evolving policy statements. Trump's Tweetstorms continue to disappoint, revolt, and even enrage Americans, like the man who took a pickax to Trump's star in Hollywood. Trump's use of Tweets even raises serious ongoing legal issues for Trump and our American legal and political system. The pros and cons of Trump's celebrity status for America is ongoing and enormously consequential.

However, consequences for ex-presidents don't always materialize as expected as these examples indicate. Even impeachment did not destroy Bill Clinton's perpetual post presidency celebrity status. Richard Nixon's resignation in disgrace did not completely hamper his celebrity status as a post presidency pundit. However, celebrity power and political power become poignant tests of wisdom, ethical integrity, humility, and even mental stability for presidents in office as well as ex-presidents.

An Array of Approaches Describing Trump's Reality TV Political Style

As I explored Trump's personality, leadership style, individual psychology, apparent motivation, and political tactics, I wrote a series of articles and papers about Trump's behavior from several points of view: allegorical, poetic, political polemical, satirical/parodic (tongue-in-cheek), a fable, literary-systemic, and concluding in psychodynamic psychoanalytic observations. This collection of articles was used because traditional applied psychoanalytic theorizing or political science approaches didn't seem to give a full or accurate picture of the elusive, unorthodox, bombastic, reality TV toned, and hyperbolic approaches to politics, political campaigning, and governing that Trump offers. Trump's political style drives traditional psychological and political science experts to distraction, irritation, histrionic speculation, or narcissistic rage. The TV and print media love to hate and lugubriously fact-check Trump as they sell newspapers and fill TV time slots.

An Allegory About Donald Trump and His Collisions with Legal and Legalistic Celebrities

The vast differences between the personalities and professional backgrounds of James Comey, Robert Mueller, Bill Barr, and Trump lead to the following irreverent extraterrestrial and interplanetary allegory. Such a fantasy can allow one possible grasp of these personality collisions.

Trump Is from Mars, Barr from Mercury, Comey from Saturn, and Mueller from Uranus

The James Comey testimony before Congress stirred US media explosions about alleged obstruction of justice by President Trump. Comey's new book, *A Higher Loyalty: Truth. Lies and Leadership*, describes Trump as a liar and morally defective. Trump was quick to do the same toward Comey who he tactlessly calls a "slime bag" among other verbal niceties. Were Martian Trump and Saturnian Comey's personalities bound to clash and then mire in profound misunderstanding? Is Robert Mueller's planet closer to Comey's than Trumps? Now a new question arises: is Barr from Mercury and closest to the Earth and down to earth?

Donald Trump, Martian

Mars is the fourth planet from the Sun and the second-smallest planet in the Solar System after Mercury. Moons: Phobos, Deimos.

Mars was a God of war (Wikipedia).

Donald John Trump attended the prestigious Wharton Business School at Penn after three years at Fordham University. However, he came up through military school at the New York Military Academy a year before Fordham, probably because of his adolescent brashness. Trump's actual halls of education were the rough and tumble world of the competitive New York construction and real estate business. Successful reality TV was another element in his postgraduate marketing education. Long Island and Brooklyn boys of his day took no guff. You could be fun and friendly, but if someone hit you physically or symbolically, you hit back and hit harder. Trump won the Republican nomination using this principal to excess. Trump also lives and breathes macho loyalty. Trump is charming, seductive, and ultimately flexible as an ultimo negotiator. If Trump hints about a favor, he does not expect you to do his wishes but he sure as hell will try to persuade you. Trump has reverence for military generals who are known to be winners. Trump's style is a mixture of flamboyance, impulsive verbosity, deal-making seductiveness, hyperbolic humor, and verbal aggression. In his marital orbit(s), Trump has had three moons: Melania, Marla, Ivana, and other likely stormy passing comets. Politically and militarily, Trump projects an image of a Martian war God.

James Comey, Saturnian

Saturn is the sixth planet from the Sun and the second largest in the solar system, after Jupiter. It is a gas giant with an average radius about nine times that of Earth. It has only one-eighth the average density of Earth, but with its larger volume Saturn is over ninety-five times more massive. Moons: Enceladus, Titan, Mimas, Dione, Tethys, Iapetus, Rhea (Wikipedia).

In Trump's sphere, along comes James Brien Comey Jr. who was raised in a traditional Catholic family but later became a United Methodist Sunday school teacher. Comey was a long-time Republican but later became a declared independent politically. His grandfather was a police officer and later police commissioner of Yonkers. Comey's father was in corporate real estate but nowhere near the rare air of Trump's wheeling and dealing New York business world.

As a college student at William and Mary, Comey was a chemistry and religion major who penned an interesting senior thesis comparing liberal theologian Reinhold Niebuhr and conservative Jerry Falwell. Comey was apparently fascinated with their propensity toward action. Both academically and in his career, Comey has a "straight arrow," "Captain Courageous" image. He even usurped Attorney General Loretta Lynch's role in condemning Hillary Clinton, and then grandiosely declared her unindictable. Like a true Saturnian, Comey is surrounded by rings of powerful law enforcement figures like Peter Stzrok, Andrew McCabe, and Robert Mueller who ran the FBI in the past. Mueller is Comey's mentor and good friend. Another one of Comey's Saturnian rings involved powerful justice department and Obama intelligence political appointees like John Brennan, Susan Rice, and James Clapper. Comey seems fascinated with his role as ever loyal pure leader spinning in the FBI's tight rings and strategically leaking their secrets. Comey has one moon in his marital orbit, wife Patrice Failor, and no likely comets. Is Comey's axis and soul stricken with **hatred of the aggressor** Trump?

Robert Mueller, Uranusian

Uranus is very cold and windy. The ice giant is surrounded by thirteen faint rings and twenty-seven small moons as it rotates at a nearly ninety-degree angle from the plane of its orbit. This unique tilt makes Uranus appear to spin on its side, orbiting the sun like a rolling ball (Wikipedia).

Robert Swan Mueller III is a lawyer who served as the sixth head of the FBI. A Republican, Mueller was appointed by President

George W. Bush who gave his original ten-year term a two-year extension, making him the longest-serving FBI director since J. Edgar Hoover. He is currently head of the special council investigation of Trump, Russian interference in the 2016 US election, and related matters.

A Princeton graduate, Mueller served as a Marine officer during the Vietnam War. He received the Bronze Star with combat "V" for heroism and a Purple Heart.

Mueller, like Comey, has spent a career in the rings, orbits. and satellites of law, criminal law, US government lawyering, and FBI service. After graduating from University of Virginia Law School (1973), Mueller worked for a law firm in San Francisco until his appointment as an Assistant US Attorney in San Francisco. Prior to his appointment as FBI Director, Mueller served as a US Attorney, as US Assistant Attorney General for the Criminal Division, and as Acting US Deputy Attorney General. Mueller is known to be a close friend and mentor of James Brien Comey Jr. and has one moon in his marital orbit, wife Ann Cabell Standish, and no likely other comets. Though greatly respected in Washington, is Mueller above being stricken with **hatred of the aggressor Trump**? His pick of many Trump-disliking Democrat lawyer staff members for his investigation raises questions. Mueller's own marginal memory capacity during hearings about his report before Congress raised serious questions.

William P. Barr, Mercurian

Mercury is the smallest and innermost planet in the Solar System. It is named after the Roman deity Mercury, the messenger of the gods. **William Pelham Barr** (born May 23, 1950) is an American attorney and a Republican. He was appointed by Donald Trump as the eighty-fifth US Attorney General. He had previously served in the position from 1991 to 1993, in the administration of George H.W. Bush. Before becoming attorney general the first time, Barr held numerous other posts within the DOJ. His father, Donald Barr, taught English literature at Columbia University before becoming headmaster of the Dalton School in Manhattan and later the Hackley School, both members of the Ivy League Prep League. Barr's father was born Jewish but later converted to Catholicism, and Barr was raised Catholic.

Barr grew up on the Upper West Side of Manhattan. After high school, Barr entered Columbia University, where he majored in government and graduated in 1971. He then did two years of graduate study at Columbia in government and Chinese studies after which he attended law school at George Washington Law School.

From 1973 to 1977, Barr was employed by the CIA. Barr served on the domestic policy staff at the Reagan White House from May 3, 1982, to September 5, 1983, with his official title being Deputy Assistant Director for Legal Policy. He was also in private practice for nine years with a Washington law firm.

Of great importance is the fact that Barr was known as a strong defender of presidential power and wrote advisory opinions justifying the US invasion of Panama and arrest of Manuel Noriega, and a controversial opinion that the FBI could enter onto foreign soil without the consent of the host government to apprehend fugitives wanted by the United States government for terrorism or drug trafficking. Barr declined a congressional request for the full opinion, but instead provided a document that "summarizes the principal conclusions." Congress subpoenaed the opinion and its public release after Barr's departure from the Justice Department showed he had omitted significant findings in the opinion from his summary document. Barr had been a close friend in Mueller's orbit of friendships but a friendship certainly having suffered perturbations and legal collisions.

Trump would inevitably collide with traditionally schooled politicians, lawyers, judges, political scientists, social scientists, academics, economists, and mostly liberal Democrat media. An analogy might involve a hypothetical, brilliant, captain navigator of sailing ships. This captain cannot read, write, or study navigation books but through vast life experience could successfully navigate through a long voyage using the stars, vast hands-on sailing experience, and leadership of a crew of sailors. Such a captain would be doubted by traditional technically trained sea captains.

Legal Celebrity Planets Collide

The ill-fated collision between Comey's and Trump's realms began at a White House meeting and a not-so-free dinner. Comey expressed fear of being alone with Trump. Trump in his usual negotiating flamboyant style expressed loyalty toward Michael Flynn who had made serious mistakes separate from his role in Trump's campaign. Trump expressed hope that Flynn, who had served America loyally, would not be excoriated by relentless legal actions. Though towering over tall man Trump, Comey testified that he felt stunned, intimidated, and unable to even tell Trump he felt uneasy with their conversation. Comey chose to make notes highly suggesting that Trump was trying to threaten his job, blackmail him, and possibly obstruct justice. Mars crashed through the rings to collide with Saturn and Washington's swamp. The American liberal media is dizzy with excitement and Watergate-style frenzy and delight. Facts and truth scatter like stardust across the American political solar system.

It was and is likely that Comey's close friend and mentor, Mueller, reacted toward Trump like a true Saturnian or even colder Uranusian. Feeling an impending fight, Trump, in usual fashion, began punching and continues to punch at Mueller with Tweets. The Trump-Comey/Mueller collision of planets is likely an unfortunate but highly consequential **Rashomon**-like event[5].

Mars trumps Saturn so far. But Uranus, cold and long-winded,

---

[5] ***The Rashomon effect*** refers to an instance when the same event is described in significantly different (often contradictory) ways by different people who were involved (Dictionary.com).

might now have trumped Trump? Now, Barr like a true Mercurian messenger of the gods, tried to come to the rescue of Trump and perhaps the basic stability of our American Republic's orbit. But Trump and Barr had their inevitable collisions and Barr resigned before January 6th, 2021.

An Irreverent Poetic Summary

Humpty Trumpty

Donald Humpty Trumpty wanted a wall,
Fake News planned Trump's downfall.
Comey, Mueller, and Schiff attackers,
Have not yet put dandy Don Trumpty in jail.
Messenger Barr, stalked by Democrats,
Stepped up to the bar speaking like a bold mensch
To whom Donald would not listen …
But, alas, used a sagaciously applied pen to resign.

AND …

A Modern American Political Fable: Anti-Androcles and the Democrat Donkeys

Once upon a modern time, an ambitious New York tycoon turned patrician politician decided to run for ultimate consul called President. Patrician dreams filled our hip hero Odysseus's mod thoughts. Along the dusty road toward Washington, he encountered many friendly smiling elephants with sore feet. Instead of feeling empathy for them and providing help and support, our hero mocked them, joked about their ugliness, size, lack of energy, and called them losers.

Our hero also came across braying donkeys with tender hooves. He treated them with even less empathy than the smiling elephants. Odysseus scorned them as plebian asses. Enraged, the donkeys brayed louder and murmured plans of revenge someday.

Mod Odysseus defeated swamp lions, poll-taking centurions, and vicious steeled sirens supported by the solicitors and sanctimonious thespians. The triumphant Consul Presidente now became a new Laius figure. He encountered Queen Jocasta, the plebeian power speaker, and Prince Oedipus, a shifty golden state attacker. The plotting of our mod hero's political demise grew grotesquely vengeful and filled with hate, deviousness, and pernicious lies.

Few smiling elephant patrician creatures rose to our hero's side and others offered only tepid support. Plebian donkeys, still simmering in their accumulated rage at mod hero, found many stages on which to cruelly deride him. Backstabbing became a spectacular modern thespian as well as a political blood sport. The only help for our modern anti-Androcles has left is the citizenry who still love him, a Dershowitzian donkey with integrity, and a shining deceased Starr of applied legal history. Viva the Republic!

AND …

Donald's Tale: A Satirical Knight of Roundtables and Dragons
Once upon a time in Queens, little Donald had a dream. Sprawling red dragon monsters robbed and pillaged the kingdom his mother and father loved dearly. Robin Hoods roamed in merry bands of *The Road to Serfdom* in the kingdom. Donald learned queen's and king's highway metro fighting weapons of tooth, claw, dagger, and sword. Accumulated wealth in coin of the realm, a firm ruling political foundation made. Donald and his woman climbed down from their golden castle. Win, win, his heart and soul pledged to victory for the people. Beaming beside his beautiful smiling bride he stood. Coin gobbling jousting opponents fell like leaves of forgotten New England fall seasons past. The throne later thrown to political winds, he quickly claimed amidst large loud crowds adoring. Rejoicing filled much of the land and certainly the wallets and

purses were swollen.

Ambushes awaited in the dark palace wings once white. Kept promises accumulated no grateful Androcles's lions in waiting. Spies in trusted entourages and ever beaming technocrats had teachery in mind. Boisterous bully pulpit warriors scorching political earth and countryside gather sycophant enemies like roadkill. Vanquished opponents returned to torment with trumped-up tribunals that tested Donald's strength again and again. Our hero's action words always come back to haunt him. His empathy, love, and kindness for his people merely expressed in tangible acts, drama, and melo-drama. Neither poetic forms accompanied Prince Donald perfor-mances nor court jesters to distract. Action words and promises built walls to protect the kingdom and brought much wealth to all the people. Life had seemed so good!

Then came the yellow plague of tiny viral warriors of death. Elec-tron microscopes showed their vicious death spikes that ravaged aging hearts and lungs. Our hero convulsed with rage at this enemy his word weapons and tongue sword could not destroy. The people blamed his blustering efforts to lead the vaccine charge and extol optimism about promised cures. A plotting rival opponent spewed his promises to the people from in a dark cave. Masks and distance from messengers became strange and effective weapons in new political battles. Appeals to social contracts became new sources of constitutional confusion. Experts confused each other with their pronouncements about the science to be followed.

Prince Donald's dream was shattered as he underestimated his charismatic power. He lost track of his peaceful leadership agenda. A *Lord of the Flies* trial allowed an unruly Judas mob to distract from a message of Donald's final appeal to a Senate that will never hear it. The vote counts were never correctly certified by Senators distracted by fear that that need not have ever existed. Senators draw political swords in their chambers. Little Donald's dreams of a comeback may be forever dashed!

Abstracts from an American Thinker *Article in Support of Trump*

Minority Opinion: From a Psychiatrist Psychoanalyst Trump Supporter

(This opinion piece was originally published in the *American Thinker* September 2, 2016).

Politician Lying

American voters usually are exposed to a variety of clever political demagoguery, obfuscations, deceptions, and a spectrum of lies from little white ones to whoppers. With Donald Trump's bombastic style, a **new glossary of terms** is needed to understand his evolving policies and predict his way of leading and governing if elected. The new glossary would include words and concepts such as bombast, showmanship, political bullying (a la LBJ, Teddy Roosevelt), sarcasm (cruel at times), puffery, braggadocio, exaggeration, overt insults, crude personal verbal attack, hyperbolic impulsive statements to focus large group attention, paradoxical intention, mixed simultaneous use of an object as symbol and reality. (I.e., an actual wall, a wall as the need for clear national boundaries and rules of behavior, and the inner psychological mindfulness that comes with ego strength). And extemporaneous free associations about the powerful emotions beneath political issues, ambivalent political relationships, and evolving policy statements. Bullying as a presidential art form was

used crudely but effectively by LBJ, Teddy Roosevelt, and Trump.
I imagine the following inner soliloquy of Donald Trump as
he decided to run for president:

> *I observe America floundering. I see the economy sputtering
> after almost eight years of Obama's incompetent leadership,
> mushrooming regulations that hamstring job creation, and
> ever-mushrooming national debt. I see bad trade deals with
> China, Mexico, and other countries that hurt America. I see
> tax policies that drive jobs and industries out of America. I see
> increasing unemployment especially of young black Americans.
> I see law and order declining especially in big urban areas like
> Chicago, Obama's hometown. I see migrants and illegal
> immigrants given government assistance as Americans go
> deeper into debt and poverty. Big expensive government pro-
> grams favored by Democrat politicians are redundant and
> often failing. I see American military power, political leader-
> ship in the world decline to the extent that other nations laugh
> at us behind our backs as they give smarmy smiles to Obama.
> The Obama administration seems bound and determined to
> teach white America and Americans in general to be ashamed
> of their/our alleged hidden racism, bigotry, Islamophobia,
> homophobia, and xenophobia. He shames us and our political
> leaders who he paints as bad guys if they disagree with him.
> The constant search for microaggressions and political incor-
> rectness by Obamaites repulses me. I watched Obama and his
> minions insult, lie about, and distort the motives, intentions,
> and character of sweet gentlemen like John McCain and Mitt
> Romney. I know I can be a strong, powerful, and benevolent
> leader to rescue America. Obama uses his sneaky phone and
> pen to bring America down a peg or two and share its/our
> wealth around in some neosocialist ways. I know and have
> participated in the rigged American political system that is

floundering. I know where the crooked bodies are buried. I made billions legally through the flawed system in America. I will be a benevolent Trojan Horse to lead a hopefully bloodless revolution in America. I will use a P.T. Barnum, applied reality TV model of politics to win. I can't be bought by anyone. America will be great and safe again. I love America so much that I will make mistakes and try to honestly correct them. I will listen to as many Americans as I can. I will talk straight to them about what I see as the truth of where America must go to be great and safe again. I will re-make the Republican party into a modern this time successful Bull Moose Populist Republican Party. Here I come, a new TR!

The Art of Verbal Attack

I notice that Trump and Hillary Clinton, and Trump and Biden viciously verbally attacked, and to this day continue to attack each other, in ways similar to John Adams and Thomas Jefferson early in our country's history. Trump is no angel and has some macho traits similar to many traditional American men. However, I think it is refreshing that Trump is defiantly politically incorrect and says what he thinks at campaign and governing free associative moments. He behaves and speaks spontaneously unlike the usual American candidate's canned talking points pretested at focus groups.

Surprisingly, I think Trump knows how to listen, is flexibly sincere about changing his mind. He is confidently unapologetic about such changes. He follows the principles of his bestseller, *The Art of the Deal,* when negotiating with Congress, foreign and community leaders.

Hiring and Firing

I think Trump, unlike typical spineless political leaders, knows how to hire, and most of all, fire, incompetent administrators. Trump will not tolerate all the "smidgens" of corruption at the IRS, the VA, and the unjust racially divisive Justice Department.

In September 2016, I thought (And still do) …
Building walls around America to form healthy strong borders is analogous to clear, firm personal boundaries that give evidence of ego strength. Trump is and can be a strong, flexible father figure who by making our streets and borders safe can help our citizens to find opportunities for individual growth and financial success. Dependency on government assistance will only be for those citizens truly unable to work and support themselves. Trump as a strong successful father figure for America will encourage Black American youths to find mentors in a safe work world, not in destructive drug gang leaders. Building a strong, well educated, and trained military will allow young Americans to serve their country in a military deserving respect and in other ways of serving America at home and abroad.

As a lonesome maverick psychoanalyst Trump supporter in the minority, I felt the need to exercise my first amendment right of free speech.

Chaos Theory, Saul Alinsky Tactics, and Donald Trump's Art of the Deal Approach to American Politics and Leadership

Donald Trump approaches American politics via an intuitive, extemporaneous, creative amalgam of Chaos Theory, Saul Alinsky Tactics, and his *The Art of the Deal*. It is unlikely that Trump consciously uses any theoretical approach, but careful study of his book is illuminating.

Chaos Theory

After relativity and quantum mechanics, chaos theory has become the twentieth century's third great revolution in physical sciences.

Definition: **chaos theory** is a mathematical theory that can be used to explain complex systems such as weather, astronomy, politics, and economics. Although many complex systems appear to behave in a random manner, chaos theory shows that there is an underlying order that is difficult to see. **Originators**: Henri Poincaré (1854-1912), Edward Lorenz (1917-2008) (LT learning theories, Internet).

Example: Edward Lorenz (1960) created a simple weather model in which small changes in starting conditions led to a marked ("catastrophic") change in outcome (called "sensitive dependence on initial conditions")—i.e., the "butterfly effect" (i.e., "the notion that a butterfly stirring the air today in Peking can transform storm systems next month in New York").

Trump and His Chaos Theory

Trump uses a derivative of chaos theory applied to business in his political behaviors. He probably does this intuitively and not from didactic reading and study. In brief, if a system is broken and dysfunctional, break it. The chaos that ensues can be used to form and develop a fix for the system. If an ambassador or cabinet member is not working out, "You're fired."

Another example: Trump's use of John Brennan's attack on Trump and accusation of treason, to counterattack Brennan by removing his top secret security clearance. The outrage and emotional US media chaos stirred by Brennan and Brennan's CIA and intel compatriots are used to break-up the deep state elitist intel system and expose enemy Brennan's political mischief.

Saul Alinsky Political Tactics

I urge the reader to examine which Alinsky rules Trump uses by unconscious intuition and conation, or even conscious calculation. I supply the list of rules below for the reader to think of further recent examples.

Alinsky's Twelve Rules for Radicals
Rule 1: "Power is not only what you have, but what the enemy thinks you have."

Power is derived from two main sources: money and people. (These are two things of which there is a plentiful supply. Government and corporations always have a difficult time appealing to people, and usually do so almost exclusively with economic arguments.)

*Trump uses Tweet-power impulsively to stir up emotions around a political power issue.

Rule 2: "Never go outside the expertise of your people."

It results in confusion, fear, and retreat. Feeling secure adds to the backbone of anyone.

*Trump uses stump speeches to brag about accomplishments and express extreme confidence.

Rule 3: "Whenever possible, go outside the expertise of the enemy."

Look for ways to increase insecurity, anxiety, and uncertainty.

*Trump uses early tough talk, insult, or exaggeration early in a negotiation, rather than rational policy statements.

Rule 4: "Make the enemy live up to its own book of rules."

If the rule is that every letter gets a reply, send 30,000 letters. You can kill them with this because no one can possibly obey all their own rules.

*Trump demands legislative action from Congress using their own rules and procedures.

Rule 5: "Ridicule is man's most potent weapon."

There is no defense. It is irrational. It is infuriating. It also works as a key pressure point to force the enemy into concessions. (Pretty crude, rude, and mean, huh? But often effective in the reality TV land of American politics.)

*Trump's Tweets show examples almost daily! "Low IQ Maxine Watters" who wants him impeached.

Rule 6: "A good tactic is one your people enjoy."

They will keep doing it without urging and come back to do more. (Radical activists, in this sense, are no different than any other human being. We all avoid "un-fun" activities, but we revel at and enjoy the ones that work and bring results.)

*Trump's stump rallies are fun, funny, and lively.

Rule 7: "A tactic that drags on too long becomes a drag."

Do not become old news. (Even radical activists get bored. So, to keep them excited and involved, organizers are constantly coming up with new tactics.)

*A Trump Tweet a day, keeps Trump's base at play.

Rule 8: "Keep the pressure on. Never let up."
Keep trying new things to keep the opposition off balance. As the opposition masters one approach, hit them from the flank with something new. (Attack, attack, attack from all sides, never giving the reeling organization a chance to rest, regroup, recover, and re-strategize.)

*Trump uses hatred of and resistance to himself to preoccupy Democrats with "Trump Derangement Syndrome."

Rule 9: "The threat is usually more terrifying than the thing itself."
Imagination and ego can dream up many more consequences than any activist. (Perception is reality. Large organizations always prepare a worst-case scenario, something that may be furthest from the activists' minds. The upshot is that the organization will expend enormous time and energy, creating in its own collective mind the direst of conclusions. The possibilities can easily poison the mind and result in demoralization.)

*Trump has his political enemies distracted and frozen into fantasies of bringing him down.

Rule 10: "If you push a negative hard enough, it will push through and become a positive."
Violence from the other side can win the public to your side because the public sympathizes with the underdog.

*Leftist Democrat threats of violence toward Trump, even by Joe Biden (Threat to beat Trump up in the schoolyard), is an example.

Rule 11: "The price of a successful attack is a constructive

alternative."
Never let the enemy score points because you are caught without a solution to the problem. (Activist organizations have an agenda, and their strategy is to hold a place at the table, to be given a forum to wield their power. So, they must have a compromise solution.)

*Trump's walls and proposals have many tangible and shifting figurative forms.

Rule 12: Pick the target, freeze it, personalize it, and polarize it."
Cut off the support network and isolate the target from sympathy. Go after people and not institutions; people hurt faster than institutions. (This is cruel, but highly effective. Direct, personalized criticism and ridicule works.)

*Trump's insults of opponents and their insults of him are legion.

Finally, I want to close this section with Professor Laurence Messner's creative extension of our topic into a view of Trump's leadership, as found in Trump's bestseller, *The Art of the Deal.*

Donald Trump's Art of the Deal Approach to American Politics and Leadership
I am indebted to Professor Lawrence F. Messner, Lt Col, USAF (Retired) who has given permission for me to include his excellent analysis of Trump in his own words with which I agree:

> ### Trump in Trump's Own Words
> I read Trump's book, *Trump, The Art of the Deal,* and made notes on what I considered insights to President Trump in his own words. Here is my compilation. I explain the context of most quotes and follow each one with a recent example from his presidency to help explain why he does what he does, but I leave it to the reader to

also use their own examples. The numbers in parenthesis are the page numbers in his book where I obtained these quotes.

Remember that Trump wrote this book in 1987, long before he became president, or even, possibly, contemplated it. Here are the quotes I find insightful:

1. In negotiations with a bank vice president regarding Trump's support of a harassed farmer who the bank was leaning on, Trump made an outrageous claim of a lawsuit he would bring on the bank. He stated, later, after getting the bank to back off, "Sometimes it pays to be a little wild." This is a tactic he uses today in negotiations with other people, entities, and countries. (3)

2. After a dispute with Mayor Koch's housing commissioner regarding the repair of the Wollman Ice Rink in NY City, which Trump repaired under budget and before the deadline, he said about the commissioner who he beat in court, "I don't hold it against people that they have opposed me. I'm just looking to hire the best talent wherever I find it." One way he does this is with his cabinet as he reappoints members for whatever reason. He simply moves on. (5)

3. Regarding his use of lawsuits to win a dispute, he said, "… the fact is that if you're right, you've got to take a stand, or people will walk over you." We see that almost daily in his attitude, negotiations with other countries, (China, NATO, N. Korea etc.) and tweets. (7)

4. "Nowadays, if your name is Donald Trump, everyone in the world seems to want to sue you." Or verbally attack him, both foe and friend alike. He seems to realize that from this quote. I suspect it does not influence his decisions that much. (7)

5. When staying in Los Angeles, Trump liked staying in the Beverly Hills Hotel, but in negotiating for its purchase he stated, "But I won't let my personal preferences affect my business judgment." In the words of ex-resident Clinton, Trump can compartmentalize. He does this with his presidential decisions as well as his dealings with NATO and other allies. (10)

6. When discussing an oil purchase with a friend, Trump decided not to do it. His friend told him he was missing out on a great opportunity, but later oil declined precipitously, and Trump's decision was vindicated. He then stated, "The experience taught me a few things. One is to listen to your gut, no matter how good something sounds on paper. The second is that you are generally better off sticking with what you know. And the third is that sometimes your best investments are the ones you don't make." I see this in his daily negotiations with corporations and other countries. His instincts guide him a lot despite advisors telling him otherwise. And, so far, his instincts have guided him wisely. (21)

7. While discussing an interview with a reporter he later stated, "Contrary to what a lot of people think, I don't enjoy doing press. I have been asked the same questions a million times now, and I do not particularly like talking about my personal life." This is evident in his war on the mainstream media, almost daily. (24)

8. He said of a political choice he made, "I'm a very practical guy." I believe he shows this in his daily actions. He is not an ideologue. (26)

9. His architect for Trump Towers was told, "I want the best, whatever it takes." This shows his desire for excellence in all his actions. His buildup of the depleted military is but one example. (30)

10. In the building of the Trump Towers, Trump tells his architect, who says the drawings "are not bad" and "We're getting there," "Well, push, John, I say. Push hard." Does this not sound like how he deals with daily issues? He is tireless and expects and demands the same from others around him. He pushes himself as hard as anyone else. (30)

11. "My style of deal-making is quite simple and straightforward. I aim extremely high, and then I just keep pushing and pushing and pushing to get what I'm after. Sometimes I settle for less than I sought, but in most cases I still end up with what I want." I think anyone can see this style being played out on the international scene, especially most recently in Europe and Asia. (30)

12. "More than anything else, I think deal-making is an ability you're born with. It's in the genes ... it's mostly about instincts ...You can take the smartest kid at Wharton ... and if he doesn't have the instincts, he'll never be a successful entrepreneur ... Moreover, most people who do have the instincts will never recognize that they do, because they don't have the courage or the good fortune to discover their potential." Trump has the genes. He was born with them and certainly has the courage, or as they say in Queens, NY, the "Chutzpah" to use them. He is not in the least lacking in self-confidence. (30)

13. "I like thinking big. I always have. To me it is very simple: if you're going to be thinking anyway, you might as well think big. Most people think small, because most people are afraid of success, afraid of making decisions, afraid of winning. And that gives people like me a great advantage." It is easy to see this type of thinking in his presidency. He has been bold and aggressive. For example, he is the first president in decades to get North Korea to return our missing in action military members from the Korean War. He has told his followers

they will get tired of winning so much. Other examples of his thinking big abound. (31)

14. In discussing his decision, as a young entrepreneur, to work in Manhattan instead of staying in Brooklyn and Queens like his father, he stated, "I wasn't satisfied just to earn a good living. I was looking to make a statement. I was out to build something monumental—something worth a big effort." This shows his desire to keep making a difference. It showed in his NATO efforts to get them to increase their defense spending and in defying everyone in not getting into Cold War 2 with Putin. These are but two recent examples of his making a big effort. (31)

15. Following up on his thinking big is this, "One of the keys to thinking big is total focus. I think of it almost as a controlled neurosis, which is a quality I have noticed in many highly successful entrepreneurs. They're obsessive, they're driven, they're single-minded and sometimes they're almost maniacal, but it's all channeled into their work. Where other people are paralyzed by neurosis, the people I am talking about are actually helped by it. I don't say this trait leads to a happier life, or a better life, but it's great when it comes to getting what you want." Can you see this trait in Trump being employed almost daily? (34)

16. "I believe in the power of negative thinking. I happen to be very conservative in business. I always go into the deal anticipating the worst. If you plan for the worst—if you can live with the worst—the good will always take care of itself." Perhaps this is his rationale in trying to get a Southern wall built. Even if he does not get everything, he may at least get something. (34)

17. "I also protect myself by being flexible. I never get too attached to one deal or one approach." This, too, can apply to his Southern wall strategy. (35)

18. "I'm a great believer in asking everyone for an opinion before I make a decision. It is a natural reflex … I ask, and I ask, and I ask, until I begin to get a gut feeling about something. And that's when I make a decision." Trump has demonstrated this time and again as he has hosted numerous groups at the White House and allowed everyone to express their opinions, in open forums in front of the mass media, before deciding. (36)

19. Regarding his war with his critics, including the mass media. "The other people I don't take too seriously are the critics—except when they stand in the way of my projects. In my opinion, they mostly write to impress each other …" (36-7)

20. Disclosing a bit of his narcissism, he says, "I always follow my own instincts, but I'm not going to kid you: it's also nice to get good reviews." When was his last one? (37)

21. "The worst thing you can possibly do in a deal is seem desperate to make it." He has demonstrated this over and over in his international relations and even with Congress. (37)

22. On the other hand, he says, "The best thing you can do is deal from strength, and leverage is the biggest strength you have. Leverage is having something another guy wants. Or better yet, needs. Or best of all, simply can't do without … Leverage: don't make deals without it" With Kim Jong Un what he can't do without may be his own survival. Thus, when Trump says things like his nuclear button is bigger than Kim's, Kim listens and believes it. (37-8)

23. "What you should never do is pay too much, even if that means walking away from a very good site." This applies to a good deal as well. (39)

24. "The point is that if you are a little different, or a little outrageous, or if you do things that are bold or controversial, the press is going to write about you. I've always done things a little differently, I don't mind controversy, and my deals tend

to be somewhat ambitious." The media have been writing about him daily, mostly negatively, largely because he won an election, he was assured he could not win and has been making outrageous statements and doing ambitious things ever since. (39)

25. Although Trump does not always act this way, he said, "The other thing I do when I talk with reporters is to be straight. I try not to deceive them or to be defensive, because those are precisely the ways most people get themselves into trouble with the press." He is certainly straight forward in his dealings with the press, but, perhaps, forgot his admonition to not be defensive. (40)

26. With regards to how he verbally frames his actions, results, and potential actions, "The final key to the way I promote is bravado … That's why a little hyperbole never hurts. People want to believe that something is the biggest and the greatest and the most spectacular. I call it truthful hyperbole. It's an innocent form of exaggeration—and a very effective form of promotion." Is this what led to his motto, "Make America Great Again"? (40)

27. People who got upset when President Bush and candidate Mitt Romney did not fight back, understand that this quote shows how Trump feels about that and is one reason he was elected. Conservatives finally had a president who stands up for himself. "Much as it pays to emphasize the positive, there are times when the only choice is confrontation. In most cases I am very easy to get along with. I am very good to people who are good to me. But when people treat me badly or unfairly or try to take advantage of me, my general attitude, all my life, has been to fight back very hard." (41)

28. "There are people—I categorize them as life's losers—who get their sense of accomplishment and achievement from trying to stop others. As far as I am concerned, if they had any real

ability, they would not be fighting me, they'd be doing something constructive themselves." This sounds like his thinking about the Democrat party and Hillary's movement to "Resist" after Trump defeated her for the presidency. (41)

29. About his economic policy, "I believe in spending what you have to. But I also believe in not spending more than you should." A lot of his projects come in under budget. An example is how he jawboned Boeing to build a new 747 as Air Force One for less than they originally planned. (42)

30. An insight to how he thinks about projects, "The point is that you can dream great dreams, but they'll never amount to much if you can't turn them into reality at a reasonable cost." This may be why he is pushing Mexico to pay, or at least, help pay for the wall. (43)

31. One reason he may not appear to let negativity upset him too much is found in this quote, "I don't kid myself. Life is very fragile, and success doesn't change that ... that's why I try not to take any of what's happened too seriously." (43)

32. Applying this quote to his own time as president, "The most important thing in life is to love what you're doing, because that's the only way you'll ever be really good at it." Trump seems to be enjoying his time as president and his results show how good he is at it. Former President Obama said Americans should get accustomed to 2 percent economic growth as that is the new norm, but as of this writing Trump's policies have created 4.1 percent growth and there are no signs of it slowing. (46)

33. Regarding his confrontational approach in life, "... even early on I tended to stand up and make my opinions known in a very forceful way. The difference now is that I like to use my brain instead of my fists. I was always something of a leader in my neighborhood ... for some reason I liked to stir things up, and I liked to test people." (49)

34. "It's not how many hours you put in, it's what you get done while you're working." This may be his ideas of being efficient, but he does both as he is a very tireless worker. (59)

35. "I'm someone who responds to people I have respect for, and I listen. Again, it is instincts, not marketing studies." Or the latest poll either. (62)

36. When discussing one way he pursues a deal, he stated, "I was relentless, even in the face of a total lack of encouragement, because much more often than you'd think, sheer persistence is the difference between success and failure." This may be a strategy he is using in getting his Southern wall built. The Mexican president is now even sounding like he may help. (99)

37. "That's just my makeup. I fight when I feel I'm getting screwed, even if it's costly and difficult and highly risky." This could be good or bad, but he admits he is a fighter. That is far more than the past conservative presidents and candidates did. I think many Americans respect him for that. They finally have a fighter on their side. (156)

38. "You don't act on an impulse – even a charitable one – unless you've considered the downside." This shows his attitude when negotiating with others. He seems to be a lot more contemplative than some give him credit for. (175)

39. When discussing a proposal, he was having with other business partners, who, in the final outcome, overruled him, Trump observed, "… but my attitude is that you can't get hurt asking." That shows an openness in negotiating that others may lack. (191)

40. Similarly, he has said, "I like to keep every option open in life …" This flexibility can be seen by some as a weakness, and others as a strength. (194)

41. "My attitude is that you do your best, and if it doesn't work, you move on to the next thing." Again, this is showing flexibility and the ability to not get bogged down in past

failures. Just move on. This is a most useful ability when dealing with politicians and foreign leaders. (197)

42. "I'm a big believer in comebacks." A good trait to have; isn't that right President Clinton? (198)

43. "If there is one thing, I have learned from dealing with politicians over the years, it is that the only thing guaranteed to force them into action is the press—or more specifically, fear of the press. You can apply all kinds of pressure, make all sorts of pleas and threats, contribute large sums of money to their campaigns, and generally it gets you nothing. But raise the possibility of bad press, even in an obscure publication and most politicians will jump. Bad press translates into potential lost votes, and if a politician loses enough votes, he will not get reelected. If that happens, he might have to go out and take a 9 to 5 job. That's the last thing most politicians want to do." This may help explain his disdain for most politicians which could work against him in getting his agenda passed. But at least he understands them. (202)

44. "Bullies may act tough, but they are really closet cowards. The only people bullies push around are the ones they know they can beat. Confront a strong, competent person, and he will fight back harder than ever. Confront a bully, and in most cases, he'll fold like a deck of cards." A good example is North Korea's Kim Jong Un. Trump confronted him and for the very first time Kim blinked and appears to be dismantling his nuclear capability. When Trump said his nuclear force was bigger than North Korea's Kim folded. (202)

45. When observing New York City's feeble attempts at getting the Wollman Ice Skating Rink repaired, he noticed workmen standing around for hours doing nothing. His thoughts were, "Now I saw it as a bigger problem at Wollman Rink: there was absolutely no one in charge. Leadership is perhaps the key to getting any job done." I could not agree more.

After being in leadership positions most of my life, and teaching it for over thirty years, I sincerely believe leadership is key to success. Trump recognizes this as well and, as President, he is leading from the front. (208)

46. "You don't reward failure by promoting those responsible for it, because all you'll get is more failure." This is very obvious to Trump and is demonstrated by the recent failures, at the top, of many of our intelligence community and Department of Justice. (213)

47. "As hard as I push, in the end I'm practical." This will help explain his possible responses in the future if he fails to get some of his agenda passed. (228)

48. "I said at the start that I do it to do it. But in the end, you are measured not by how much you undertake, but by what you finally accomplish." This could be his epitaph if he fails, or his legacy if he accomplishes much of his agenda. (235)

49. "I don't go out of my way to be cordial to enemies." While many think he did just that with Putin at their summit, many forget that Trump said before the summit that Putin was not an "enemy" but rather a "competitor." Since he did not see Putin as an enemy, he was cordial. (238)

50. "The biggest challenge I see over the next twenty years is to figure out some creative ways to give back some of what I've gotten … To me, what matters is the doing, and giving time is far more valuable than just giving money … One of the challenges ahead is how to use those skills as successfully in the service of others as I've done, up to now, on my own behalf." This could help explain why he ran for president. He was attempting to find a creative way to give back to America and Americans some of what he has gotten in life. (242)

Note: All quotes have been taken from *Trump: The Art of the Deal*; Donald J. Trump with Tony Schwartz; 1987. Random House, NY.

Summary and Conclusions About Trump's Style and Approaches to Political Leadership

My old friend and retired professor of Leadership studies, Lt. Col. Laurence F. Messner, says it well:

> President Trump is not an easy person to understand, comprehend or even like. I think he is more complex than most other leaders as he obliterates the norms of behavior time and again. He seems either ignorant of his tactics' impact, or perhaps he does and deliberately uses them and does not care. I think, in some ways, he is single minded. He wants to succeed as a person and for any organization he is in charge of. Now that organization is bigger and more complicated than any he has led before. A country, both in geographic size and diversity of people, beliefs and cultures, can be overwhelming for any single leader (Messner, Personal communication).

Messner adds comments about Trump and foreign affairs, with which I agree:

> I believe President Trump is obnoxious many times, but that is style. His substance is what I focus on. We have had past Republican presidents and candidates who were

less obnoxious, and they got us little in return in terms of world politics. President Trump is a consummate deal maker who sizes up his opponents quite well. He knows Xi and Kim Jong Un and while he does not trust them, he flatters them and appeals to their egos to make a deal that is best for America and the free world. I'd rather have President Trump making our country's foreign deals than anyone else (Messner, personal communication.).

Donald Trump approaches American politics in a manner that can be described by descriptive applications of Chaos Theory, Saul Alinsky Tactics, and Trump's *The Art of the Deal*. Trump's approaches befuddle traditional politicians, university academics, political pundits, print and TV journalists, reporters, and editorialists. Trump is called mentally ill and dangerous by some psychiatrists, psychologists, psychoanalysts, and other mental health professionals. The author believes that Trump not only uses the approaches previously described intuitively, extemporaneously, and not formally informed by academic approaches, but also preferably from his real world rough-and-tumble world of business, real estate, and reality TV experience. Many of Trump's attackers in the media, academia, psychiatry, psychology, and psychoanalysis, could benefit from reading carefully and understanding Saul Alinsky and Trump's *The Art Of The Deal.*

Trump's Political Style

American voters are usually exposed to a variety of clever political demagoguery, obfuscations, deceptions, and a spectrum of lies from little white ones to whoppers by politicians. With Donald Trump's bombastic style, as I have said previously, a **glossary of terms** is needed to understand his evolving policies and predict his way of leading and governing. The new glossary would include words and concepts such as bombast, puffery, braggadocio, sarcasm (cruel at times), overt insults, crude personal verbal attack, hyperbolic impulsive statements to focus large group attention, paradoxical intention in the media, mixed simultaneous use of an object as symbol and reality. (I.e., an actual wall, a wall as needed for clear individual and national boundaries and rules of behavior.) None of these words are found in the lexicon of what the American press calls "Presidential."

Trump's Style's Connection to His Narcissism and Charisma

As I have said previously, Trump's obvious narcissism is a prominent thread within the complex skein of his remarkable ego strength and aggressive personality. A strong ego is not egotistical in the common sense usage of the expression "big ego," but indicates accurate intuition, street-smart intelligence, and good judgment. Trump's extensive experience in using TV media (*The Apprentice*) with showmanship, applying Saul Alinsky by intuition, and his *Art of the Deal* establishes a unique and powerful charisma like that of powerful cult leaders. Such powerful charisma easily intimidates, infuriates, and is misunderstood by the liberal anti-Trump media. At times Trump himself seems to underestimate and misunderstand the power of his own charisma. The tragedy of the Proud Boys, and minority number of lawbreaking violent Trump supporters on January 6th, 2021, is an instance of this sad fact.

Trump, however, is strong and charismatic enough to withstand the attacks of bitter Democrats who never thought Trump would win the presidency. Strong enough to take on "the swamp" of Washington politics, politically correct liberal university professor enemies, and a massively anti-Trump and vicious liberal American press. As Trump implied early in his first campaign, he knows personally where all the political bodies are buried in Washington, how the pay-to-play swamp game is negotiated, and deals are made.

Our American president is not our country's psychiatrist, large group therapist, social worker, or pastor. He is primarily our chief executive, national and international leader and policymaker, commander-in-chief, signer, and chief enforcer of our laws, who makes important appointments.

Donald Trump is a flawed but effective person, with a flagrantly unorthodox political style.

Donald Trump's Parental and Family Psychodynamics (Psychological and Other Considerations)

As a psychiatrist and psychoanalyst, I want to offer thoughts, observations, and opinions about Donald Trump and his family. I use a negative-toned journalistic article and a psychoanalyst colleague's negatively slanted opinions about Donald Trump and his parents to offer more positive opinions and conclusions about Donald Trump. I highlight Trump's effective compensatory separation-individuation processes he used to individuate as his own person in a wealthy competitive family, yet his ability to both stand with his father and by himself, in rough and tumble, successful, and unsuccessful businesses.

Trump's Father, Mother, and Psychological Speculations About Trump's Personal and Family Psychodynamics

During my work with a person in psychoanalysis, I would frequently imagine that my analysand's mother, father, grandparents, relatives, significant schoolteachers, neighbors, and family friends were all or individually sitting quietly in my office as I listened to my patient or analysand describe thoughts, somatic sensation descriptions, associations, and dreams. My patient and I would discuss these important persons in their childhood as still influential presences in their mind in the present. My patient would accept, value, reject, devalue, laugh, cry, express anger, hatred, love, affection about the working memory presence of these persons in their mind. It is helpful to think and reflect this way about Donald Trump's family. Though some critics are harshly critical about psychiatrists and psychoanalysts' over-generalizations and often erroneously perceived blaming of parents, there can be no doubt about the important influence of parents, family, and other mentoring and role-modeling presences or absence of them in any person's life or destiny.

Donald Trump's Father

I have assembled a sketch of condensed and selected information about Fred Trump, his marriage, and family business life. Fred linked his business world with his son Donald whose businesses benefitted from the family loyalties and connections with his father. Many businesses have the titles, "father and son." From material I found in Wikipedia, Fred and Donald Trump became entwined in complex but successful ways in the rigors of the New York building, construction, and real estate world. I hope my effort conveys the difficulty in presenting facts about some of the business intricacies, potential legal pitfalls, and psychosocial dynamics in the rough and tumble business and social world of the Trump family in New York. Some of the "facts" have as yet to be established to this day. I have no expertise to assess conclusively the financial, legal, and ethical issues described below. I do think the descriptions help frame some of my psychological observations, speculations, and psychodynamic opinions and conclusions about the elusive mind and personality of Donald Trump and his family.

Frederick Christ Trump (October 11, 1905 – June 25, 1999)

Donald Trump's father Fred was an American real estate developer and builder in New York City. Frederick Christ Trump was born on October 11, 1905. When Fred was twelve years old, his father died in the 1918 Pandemic. After high school, Trump obtained full-time work pulling wagonloads of building materials to construction sites.

He continued his education at Pratt Institute. Frederick's mother Elizabeth Christ Trump signed with him to start a business because he was still a minor. The development company was incorporated as Elizabeth Christ Trump and Son in 1927. Two years after his graduation, he finished his first house in Woodhaven, Long Island, and he then built twenty more homes in Queens. The company grew to build and manage single-family houses in Queens, barracks, and garden apartments for US Navy personnel near East Coast shipyards and more than twenty-seven thousand apartments in New York. By the mid-1930s he built one of the first modern supermarkets in the city, selling customer-collected goods. After six months, Trump sold it to the King Kullen supermarket chain.

Fred Trump's 1927 Arrest

On Memorial Day in 1927, the KKK marched in Queens to protest Protestant American citizens being assaulted by Roman Catholic police of New York City. Trump and six other men were arrested on a charge of refusing to disperse from a parade when ordered to do so. Trump was the only one not held on charges. When asked about the issue in September 2015, Donald Trump then a candidate for president, denied that his father had ever been arrested.

Personal Life

Fred Trump met his future wife Mary Anne McLeod, an immigrant from Scotland, at a party in the 1930s. Trump told his mother the same evening that he had met his future wife. Trump, a Lutheran, married Mary, a Presbyterian. They had five children: Maryanne Trump Barry, born 1937 and a federal judge until her retirement; Fred Trump Jr. (1938–1981); Elizabeth Trump Grau (born 1942); Donald Trump, born 1946, the 45th president of the United States; and Robert Trump, (1948–2020), a top executive of the Trump property management company.

Fred Trump, as a father, was known as an autocrat with high expectations of success and winning. As a parent, he had curfews and forbade cursing, lipstick for his daughters, and snacking between meals. At the end of his day, Fred apparently would receive a report from Mary on the children's actions, and, if necessary, decide upon disciplinary actions. (A scenario not atypical among those of us traditionally raised in middle and upper middle class in Queens, New York, in those days). Fred took his children to building sites to collect empty bottles to return for the deposits. The boys had paper routes, and when weather conditions were poor, their father would let them make their deliveries in a limousine.

During World War II, Fred Trump built barracks and garden apartments for US Navy personnel near major shipyards along the East Coast. After the war, he expanded into middle-income housing for the families of returning veterans in the Long Island area. He made millions of dollars.

Profiteering Investigations

In early 1954, President Eisenhower and other federal leaders began denouncing real estate profiteers. On June 11, 1954, *The New York Times* included Trump on a list of thirty-five city builders accused of profiteering from government contracts.

Trump and others were investigated by a Senate Banking Committee for questionable windfall profit-taking. In testimony, investigator William McKenna cited Trump as an example of how profits were made by builders using the Federal Housing Administration. According to McKenna, Fred Trump, and partner William Tomasello obtained loans for $3.5 million more than the Beach Haven apartments had cost. On July 12, 1954, Trump argued that because he had not withdrawn the money, he had not pocketed the profits. He further testified that due to rising costs, he would have had to invest more than the 10 percent of the loan not provided by the FHA, and therefore suffer a loss if he had built under those conditions.

In 1966, Trump was again investigated for windfall profiteering, this time by New York's State Investigation Commission. After Trump overestimated building costs sponsored by a state program, he profited $598,000 on equipment rentals in the construction of Trump Village, which was then spent on other projects. Under testimony on January 27, 1966, Trump said that he had personally done nothing wrong and praised the success of his building project. The commission called Trump "a pretty shrewd character" with a "talent for getting every ounce of profit out of his housing project." No indictments were made. Instead, tighter administration protocols and accountability in the state's housing program were called for by the commission.

Donald Trump Joined His Father in The Trump Company

Donald Trump joined Trump Management Company in 1968, and he rose to become company president in 1971. In the mid-1970s, Donald received loans from his father exceeding $14 million (later claimed by Donald to have been $1 million). This allowed Donald to enter the real estate business in Manhattan, while his father remained in business in Brooklyn and Queens. "It was good for me," Donald Trump later commented. "You know, being the son of somebody, it could have been competition to me. This way, I got Manhattan all to myself." It could be argued that this was healthy competition benefitting both Fred and son Donald. Fred Trump helped his son with several significant loans.

A Complex Civil Rights Legal Confrontation

Minority applicants turned away from renting Trump apartments complained to the New York City's commission on human rights and the Urban League, leading the League and other groups to send test applicants to Trump-owned complexes in July 1972. They concluded that whites were offered apartments, while blacks were generally steered away. Both of the aforementioned advocacy organizations then raised the issue with the Justice Department. In October 1973, the Civil Rights Division of the DOJ filed a civil rights suit against the Trump Organization (Fred Trump, chair, and Donald Trump, president) for infringing the Fair Housing Act of 1968. In response, Trump attorney Roy Cohen countersued for $100 million by implicating the DOJ for alleged false accusations.

Court records showed that four landlords or rental agents confirmed that applications sent to the Trump organization's head office for approval denoted the race of the applicant. A rental agent said that Fred Trump had instructed him "not to rent to blacks" and to "decrease the number of black tenants by encouraging them to locate housing elsewhere." A Consent Decree between the DOJ and the Trump Organization was signed on June 10, 1975, with both sides claiming victory—the Trump Organization for its perceived ability to continue denying rentals to welfare recipients, and the head of DOJ's housing division for the decree being far-reaching. It personally and corporately prohibited the Trumps from "discriminating against any person in the ... sale or rental of a dwelling," and "required Trump to advertise vacancies in minority papers, promote minorities to professional jobs, and list vacancies on a preferential basis." Finally, it ordered the Trumps to "thoroughly acquaint themselves personally on a detailed basis with ... the Fair Housing Act of 1968." The author would suggest that in that time in American history, Trump and successful real estate entrepreneurs were appropriately and importantly educated as America's important progress in racial progress was occurring. Harsh critics of the Trumps could describe the situation in less favorable ways.

Wealth and Estate

Fred Trump appeared on the Forbes Four Hundred list of Richest Americans in 1982 with an estimated $200 million fortune shared with his son Donald. In 1976, Trump had set up trust funds of $1 million for each of his five children and three grandchildren that paid out yearly dividends. By 1993, the siblings' anticipated shares of Trump's estate amounted to $35 million each. Upon Trump's death in 1999, his will divided $20 million after taxes among his surviving children.

In October 2018, *The New York Times* published an exposé drawing on more than 100,000 pages of tax returns and financial records from Trump's businesses, and interviews with former advisers and employees. *The Times* concluded that his son Donald "was a millionaire by age 8," and that he had received $413 million (adjusted for inflation) from Fred's business empire over his lifetime. According to *The Times*, Trump loaned at least $60 million to his son, who largely failed to reimburse him. **Another view of the situation would be that "Trump and Son" businesses had been a mutually profitable domain in a complex rough and tumble New York business arena!** The paper also described a number of purportedly fraudulent tax schemes; for example, when Trump sold shares in Trump Palace condos to his son well below their purchase price, thus masking what could be considered a hidden donation, and benefiting from a tax write-off. Donald Trump's lawyer denied the allegations of fraud and tax evasion, while the New York tax department stated they would investigate the issue. **The author would raise the issue about whether the "Fake News" *New York Times* attacks on Donald Trump began as Trump has alluded to many decades ago and continues in bitter tones back and forth today!** Americans pick a side. The author would contend that Donald Trump learned valuable information and had important tangible experience not in the academic environment of a master's or PHD degree in business or law school, but in the real world just described.

Philanthropy

Fred and Mary Trump supported medical charities by donating buildings. After Mary received medical care at the Jamaica Hospital Medical Center, they donated the Trump Pavilion to the Jamaica

Hospital Medical Center. Fred was also a trustee of the hospital. The couple donated a two-building complex in Brooklyn as a home for "functionally retarded adults" and other buildings to the National Kidney Foundation of New York and New Jersey. The Cerebral Palsy Foundation of New York and New Jersey also received a building. In addition, Fred made charitable contributions to the Long Island Jewish Hospital and the Hospital for Special Surgery in Manhattan.

The Trumps were active in the Salvation Army, the Boy Scouts of America, and the Lighthouse for the Blind. Fred also supported the Kew-Forest School where his children attended, and he served on the board of directors. Trump was active in Jewish and Israeli causes. This included donating the land for the Beach Haven Jewish Center in Flatbush, New York. Fred supported Israel Bonds and served as the treasurer of an Israel benefit concert featuring American performers. During the 1980s, Fred Trump became friends with future Prime Minister of Israel, Benjamin Netanyahu, who, at the time, was the Israeli Ambassador to the United Nations.

Donald Trump and His Father

Justin Frank discusses the relationship between Donald Trump and his father at length. Frank extrapolates from Fred Trump Senior's obsession with work, financial success, competing, and winning to conclude, and probably accurately, that Fred Trump was often absent from Donald's daily life as a boy. Because Fred was also a strict disciplinarian, the combination left Donald without a consistent paternal presence to help regulate his aggression. This led to both "father hunger" for young Donald and also acting out and bullying behavior. Some of these connections are well described by Dr. Justin Frank in his book about Trump. Frank makes a big issue about Fred Trump's "exiling" Donald to military school. As I argued earlier, rather than a major traumatic rejection of Donald by his father, this step could have been Fred's recognition that the military school could provide more structure and channeling of young Donald's aggression that Fred could not offer for various reasons. It is noteworthy that Donald Trump reveres the military and father figures like Jim Mattis, "Mad Dog" as Trump liked to call Mattis; but Trump also was able to fire Mattis when they differed over issues like NATO funding and dealing with our allies. Trump also is eager to have a strong military but seeks to bring troops home and away from endless wars overseas. Fred Trump, like all of us fathers of sons, struggled and made many mistakes, some very painful.

Fred Trump Senior's Later Years and Death

Fred Trump and his wife were given an apartment on the fifty-fifth floor of Trump Tower, which they rarely used. Fred Trump died in 1999. He suffered from Alzheimer's disease for the last six years of his life, finally dying of pneumonia at ninety-three. He is buried in Queens, New York. His widow, Mary, died a year later on August 7, 2000. Mary Trump was eighty-eight years old.

Donald Trump's Mother

Nina Burleigh, a Newsweek national politics correspondent, did a fascinating and perceptive article about Donald Trump's mother, Mary Anne MacLeod. Though unflattering toward Donald Trump himself, it provides helpful background toward trying to understand his personality dynamics vis-à-vis his mother's influence. I am indebted to Burleigh's careful and detailed journalistic work in helping my psychodynamic approach to understanding Donald Trump's mother's influence on Trump's personality.

Burleigh points out that Mary Anne MacLeod's fellow parishioners at the Stornoway High Church on the Isle of Lewis in Scotland remember the dignified blonde who came back to Isle of Lewis from America every summer. They described Mary Anne as walking with a formal, erect posture. Some whispered about how she had picked up "airs and graces" in New York, where she had married a rich man. They were impressed, however, with her speaking Gaelic as though she had never left the island. They were amazed at the mother of Donald Trump, the aggressive rich kid turned real estate mogul turned President of the United States. Burleigh thinks Mary MacLeod's life journey is a key to understanding Trump's deep insecurity—or, in my opinion, Donald Trump's restless ambition to work hard, transcend limitations and succeed.

MacLeod spent the first seventeen years of her life in Tong, a fishing village on the Isle of Lewis. In the Outer Hebrides, it is closer to Iceland than to London. Though Donald Trump was raised in a mansion in Queens, New York, Mary Anne MacLeod grew up among poor islanders in a two-bedroom rented cottage with her ten siblings.

The MacLeods lived several miles from their church, on a tidal flat, "the saltings." Often, the muck turned into quicksand. To get to church on Sunday the family would pick their way across the flats in muck boots. It was a perilous journey that only fishing families would even attempt because people could drown. On weekdays, MacLeod's family worked hard, digging peat to burn, hauling fishing nets in the icy rain, and farming meager crops they grew in the rocky soil.

An English opium baron named Matheson had purchased the entire island of Lewis in the mid-nineteenth century and built himself a gray stone Victorian castle on a plot of land overlooking Stornoway. The MacLeod family's church was on Matheson Road, a street lined with small but handsome brick mansions belonging to the families of local merchants. To distinguish themselves from their impoverished neighbors, residents of these mansions forbade the poor to walk on their street. That ban would have included MacLeod and her family.

In Mary's grandparents' generation, the British had expelled tens of thousands of Scottish peasants in order to empty the land for sport hunting and sheep. Many emigrated to North America, on ships whose conditions were so bad that many perished of scurvy and other ailments before they reached land. Those remaining clung to farming, fishing, and spoke Gaelic at church and school. Their English overlords tried to force their language upon them. MacLeod, for instance, did not hear much English until she enrolled in school, which was compulsory only until eighth grade.

Mary was only seven when World War I ended. The war and a local maritime disaster, a winter shipwreck just yards from shore, killed two hundred soldiers returning from the front, decimating the male population. The shortage of men, and the promise of a better life in America, prompted Mary to join her older sisters in New York in 1929. Her sisters were married to butlers and worked as maids or servants. They got Mary a job when she arrived. All the MacLeod siblings eventually emigrated to North America, except one who remained behind and took care of the parents. The exodus from Lewis was overly dramatic in MacLeod's generation.

The men left behind grew fed up with aristocratic landowners and staged a series of raids to seize what British authorities had promised them if they fought in World War I, their own land. Landowners gave in and granted back property to the tenant farmers in the community. Modern day island families living on this land pay rent to a public trust, not English lords. At a collective unconscious level, Trump, like men in his mother's clan, relished **a good fight to be won at all costs.**

Six years after she arrived in New York, MacLeod, the blue-eyed youngest member of her family, met a blonde, mustachioed, first-generation German American at a party in Queens. They married and Fred Trump became one of the biggest and wealthiest home builders in suburban Queens, New York. Mary then spent her adult years recreating the pomp she had only viewed from the proverbial window as a girl. Despite her lack of education and lowly roots, Mary apparently liked to wear furs and be chauffeured in a Rolls Royce around New York. Donald Trump wrote about his mother's passion for the trappings of wealth, such as being enthralled by the coronation of Queen Elizabeth. Donald Trump has been attracted to beautiful, accomplished women of independence, grit, and confidence who will not be underestimated. His mother set a psychological stage for this domain of romance.

Nina Burleigh speculates perceptively that Donald Trump inherited his mother's obsession with the trappings of class and luxury and an insecurity about not being born to the wealthy elite. Burleigh observes that Trump built himself a miniature Versailles, his gold and marble triplex in Trump Tower. It was designed by another immigrant with queenly tastes, first wife Ivana Trump. And perhaps because his mother left Scotland with less than a high school education, Trump has defended her obliquely by scoffing about book-learning and pretentious people with academic degrees. Donald Trump said in his book, "The most important thing I learned at Wharton was not to be overly impressed by academic credentials," Trump also wrote in *The Art of the Deal.* "It didn't take me long to realize that there was nothing particularly awesome or exceptional about my classmates, and that I could compete with them just fine." Trump has, at times, thumbed his nose at old money New Yorkers who did not like his buildings. One could say in a positive way that Donald Trump's outspoken, iconoclastic, independent, and street-smart rebellious style represents an unconscious identification with his mother. There are other more important smarts than book-based smarts.

Mary MacLeod, however, never turned her back on her roots. According to Burleigh, she always returned to Tong, year after year, lapsing into Gaelic the minute she arrived. The islanders cite the Gaelic saying "The bird sings best in its nest" to explain her attachment. Donald Trump, though, never came with her, which probably reflected unconscious ambivalence.

Today, the peat fields are still part of the island's landscape, but residents are more connected to the rest of the world. The people of Lewis were amused and proud of their American son, Donald, when they first learned he was a reality TV celebrity. But after he strong-armed mainland Scots near Aberdeen into land concessions for his "best golf course in the world," and as his political career grew, many in his mother's hometown grew ashamed of him—according to Burleigh.

Donald Trump apparently visited Tong only once while he was in Scotland while inspecting work on his golf course in 2008. At the MacLeod cottage, Trump said he felt Scottish. A relative of Donald Trump has said he is a rabble rouser in the mode of that *Apprentice* thing. The relative called him outrageous and opined that Mary MacLeod would be horrified about her now famous son. Horrified, or surprised and impressed, by a lovely resilient woman like her handsome, tenacious son Donald? Such may be the stuff of how "fake news" is generated or a hint at one psychological dynamic about how Trump's audacious, flamboyant, and outspoken mother is like her outspoken son. Two tough, determined, and resilient cookies!

*Reference: NEWSWEEK, Nina Burleigh, National Politics Correspondent On 12/28/17

Justin Frank, MD, in his psycho-biographic study of Donald Trump, *Trump on the Couch*, **theorizes about Trump's mother Mary**. On page 4 (dark highlighting is mine) of Frank's book about Trump, Frank says:

> We can hope that future historians and biographers will more closely examine Trump's life story to gain further insight into the events of his formative years that con-tributed to the development of **a character so pro-foundly lacking in the attributes appropriate for the office** he was so tenaciously compelled to pursue (Frank, p4).

Justin Frank emphasizes a picture of Mary Trump as psychologically absent, disengaged, remote, and enthralled by Queen Elizabeth. Frank speculates, along with internet sleuths, that even Donald Trump's hairstyle, "shares an assertive disregard for both gravity and natural color with the style his mother wore." Frank audaciously asks if Donald is trying to recreate or elicit the loving maternal gaze he missed out on as an infant. Another interpretation could be that Donald, like Mary, mobilized a sense of grit and determination to rise above mediocrity and strive for regal quality and station in life through social artistic architectural endeavor. I would ask: had Frank made political conclusions before exploring his Kleinian psychoanalytic observations and conclusions about Trump's personality and character? Such is the danger of any psychoanalytic conclusions about celebrities or notorious persons that we as psychoanalysts have never examined over the course of many interviews with that person. The "data" Frank presents in his Kleinian conclusions drawn from Trump interviews—Trump's books such as, *Art of The Deal* and other sources not exactly friendly toward Trump—can be interpreted in other ways. I will describe different interpretations from other psychoanalytic theorists and my perspective as a Freudian trained psychoanalyst strongly influenced by the ideas of noted psychoanalysts Otto Kernberg and Heinz Kohut, and my own applied psychoanalytic experience.

Many Psychoanalytic Opinions Could Cluster Around Donald Trump and His Parents: A Brief Summary

A **Kleinian** psychoanalyst, Justin Frank, focused on his intuitions and informed speculations about Donald Trump's early childhood relationship with his mother and its lifelong consequences for Trump's personality. Likely some of these psychodynamic areas are relevant but only a part of a complex domain. A **Freudian** psychoanalyst might quickly focus on the oedipal triangle of Donald, his mother Mary, and his father Fred. This triangle's flavor is often a relevant domain in middle class and upper middle-class American families, especially in Queens, New York, where I grew up. Fathers were often away for long days working hard, striving hard to successfully provide for their family. They sought prestige and social stature for themselves and their family. Mothers were immersed in full-time homemaker roles or were administrators of maids and servants who took care of the children, and they took part in community and charitable activities as did Mary Trump.

Was Mary Trump seeking to rise above her childhood of poverty and through her beauty marry a successful wealthy man in order to achieve her queenly or princess fantasies of royalty, grace, and success? Quite likely. Was Fred Trump smitten with a special beauty queen or princess of his young man dreams? I think yes. Did Fred and Mary fancy their children as part of a fantasied royal family that a **Jungian** psychoanalyst might explore as a heroic architype of royalty dreams of power and glory? Did they both reluctantly but secretly value the dreamworld status that their son Donald achieved as the most powerful man in the world, in Fred's words a "killer and winner"? Very likely if Fred were alive today. And in Mary's words, "What kind of son have I created?" Likely, but the meaning of Mary's statement is up to the reader to decide. I think she would have been impressed with her son the president's long cordial visit with Queen Elizabeth.

Would **Kernberg** raise questions about Trump's repression or denial about his own aggression toward both his parents and others? I think, yes. Would **Kohut** have questioned Trump's defects in empathy, especially for those who oppose him or criticize him? Yes, but I would observe that Trump's creativity with sarcasm and humor shows higher transformations of narcissism.

In my opinion, Donald Trump was loved as best Fred and Mary Trump were able to love. I also think Donald Trump struggled to separate and individuate from his parents psychologically as best he could on his life journey. He, in my opinion, successfully transcended each of his parent's neurotic personality struggles and parental blind spots. In addition, I think Trump **compensated** successfully for his childhood reading and learning difficulties in creative ways. He both failed and succeeded in a rough and tumble business world, the dynamics of which few people fully understand. Trump seems particularly misunderstood by many psychiatrists, academicians, journalists, political scientists, and, especially, career politicians and government bureaucrats. Since we have no authentic psychoanalytic data or any real density of applied psychoanalytic data about Trump, I would prefer to take Donald Trump in his own words as Justin Frank quotes him when Trump said this about his parents in Trump's self-help book, *Think Big: Make it Happen in Business and in Life*:

> She wanted me to be happy. My father understood me more and he said, "I want you to be successful." He was a very driven kind of guy. That's why I am so screwed up, because I had a father that pushed me pretty hard. My father was a tough man, but he was a good man, and he would always tell me to do something that you love. Now I am happy, so I ended up doing what both my parents wanted me to do" (Frank, pp20-21).

I disagree with Frank. When Trump refers to himself as "screwed up" it is not a pathological slip of the tongue at a Q&A interview, but Trump's playful self-disparaging sense of humor.

Donald Trump and His Brother Fred Trump Jr.

As I said at the beginning of my book, Fred Trump Junior died in 1981 of a heart attack and alcoholism. Fred Trump Senior had abnormally high expectations of success and winning at all costs for all his children and clearly for himself and his spouse. He even used the expression "Be a killer" as an expression to spur on his sons. In addition, Fred Trump Senior was so consumed with his business's success that he seemed to fuse his family's destiny with that of The Trump Building and real estate company ventures.

Feeling the namesake focused pressure, Fred Trump Jr. recoiled against Trump Inc. and pushed toward his ambition to be an airline pilot. Donald Trump chose, and was chosen, to join with his father and the company. Unfortunately, in the process it appears that Fred Trump Jr. felt both pressure not to follow his bliss in flying but also a sense of rejection from his father for so doing. On one occasion, Fred Trump Sr. angrily put down Fred Jr's ambition to be an airline pilot as like being a bus driver in the sky. Donald, who was present, did not defend his brother on that occasion.

Donald Trump, regardless of the presence of sibling rivalry dynamics, chose to enthusiastically embrace and merge with his father's company and made it a key part of his own career trajectory.

Alcoholism has no single cause. However, Donald Trump, who admired his brother Fred's handsomeness and intelligence, described at interviews the profound effect his brother Fred's destructive drinking had on him. Donald Trump expressed the regret (perhaps shame) he felt for, I assume, the part he might have played in pressures on Fred Jr. in the family business. Actually, Fred Trump Senior had openly derided Fred Jr. as a loser in comparison to Donald. Fred Jr. reached his goal of becoming a pilot for TWA, but sadly, it was short-lived because he was fired due to his alcoholism.

Donald Trump in a "turning-of-lemons-to-lemonade" type dynamic told journalists that seeing his brother destroyed by alcoholism helped shape his presidential administration's attempts to make efforts to take on the problems of alcohol and opioid addiction. Trump, in fact, donated one hundred thousand dollars of his presidential salary toward alcoholism research. Fred Jr's alcoholism also led Donald Trump never to use alcohol and a conviction that he has genetic susceptibility toward alcohol addiction. Such a choice on Trump's part indicates his wisdom and **ego strength**[6].

Donald Trump's Niece: Mary L. Trump's Perspective on Her Uncle

I choose to discuss Mary L. Trump's opinion about her uncle Donald Trump for several reasons. She has had professional training in psychology and psychotherapy. Her education and training in psychology includes the important element of caution that writing about a family member in the manner that she has done is unprofessional and possibly unethical. The content of her book indicates the depth of strong feelings and antipathy she feels towards President Trump for apparent financial and related reasons of many intense family conflicts. Despite, and/or perhaps because of the above factors, Mary L. Trump's descriptions have some applied psychological value for this, my book about *The Misunderstood Mind of Donald Trump*.

Dr. Mary L. Trump's book is called *Too Much and Never Enough: How My Family Created the World's Most Dangerous Man*. I have not read the book, but journalists Alan Feuer, Michael Rothfeld, and Maggie Haberman[7] have published an extensive and painfully detailed article about the financial, unhappy, conflicted, emotional, and endlessly unsettling legal paradoxes and conundrums Dr. Mary Trump describes about the Trump family, **her family**. The article, and I am sure the book, makes for intensely dramatic but profoundly sad reading.

Dr. Mary Trump has an informative view of what she regards as a highly dysfunctional "neurotic" Trump family. The term neurotic, just like narcissistic, is not a psychiatric or psychoanalytic curse

---

[6] **Ego strength** signifies to psychoanalysts the executive function of the human mind that helps us maintain emotional stability and cope with internal and external stress. It should not be confused with the common parlance use of the term "a big ego" implying a pathological narcissism or selfishness!

[7] Alan Feuer, Michael Rothfeld, and Maggie Haberman, "The Inside Story of Why Mary Trump Wrote a Tell-All Memoir," *The New York Times*. New York City. Archived from the original on July 8, 2020.

word. We psychoanalysts, of all people, should be the last to cast the first psychological interpretive stone about the pain of neurotic conflict in individuals, couples, families, or ourselves! We on couches during our own training analyses and in our work with our patients, certainly know this fact. If we extend our empathy to Mary Trump and every member of her family, we can learn from her descriptions. Even if every one of her clinical conclusions are true about our president and the Trump family dysfunctions—and they are not—they offer a distorted but painful piece of the puzzle of understanding Donald Trump's mind.

Donald Trump's Biopsychological Educational Developmental Issues— All His Own

Justin Frank provides fascinating, provocative, and evocative observations of what he calls, "worrisome disorders" of Donald Trump's thought and language on pages 206-226 of his book, *Trump on the Couch.*

Frank presents accurately clinically worded descriptions of what he thinks are Donald Trump's significant, cognitive limitations (tangential thinking, oblique responses, and deflections in thought responses); possible early onset Alzheimer's symptoms like empty adjectives and phrase repetitions; indications of a subtype of dyslexia; learning disability; binary thinking and paramnesias. These residual mental traits are traced partially to Trump's postulated childhood learning disorder, reading disorder, and hyperactivity. Frank's postulations about Trump's childhood have some truth, but extrapolation to Trump's current mental functioning is more than a stretch! Frank, on page 137, even states an absurd and snarky question, "Which prospect is more frightening to Donald Trump, revealing his tax returns or starting a nuclear war?" To attribute such dangerousness to President Trump is professionally irresponsible.

Some Conclusions About Donald Trump's Psyche

I postulate that Trump has successfully compensated for the alleged childhood developmental hurdles that Frank describes. Donald Trump's personality is a tangled skein of ego strength, resilience, and a successfully **compensated**[8] pattern of phallic aggressive, hypomanic, and narcissistic personality traits. Trump uses defense mechanisms such as externalization, denial, and projection, which are regarded by many psychoanalysts as less healthy defenses. Such cerebrally oriented psychoanalysts would seem to prefer that Trump use intellectualization, sublimation, rationalization, and Kleinian depressive defensive positions.

Trump is a man of action as primary, then words arrive. His creativity takes the form of careful street-smart intuition-based listening, followed by effective actions. He is psychologically **compensated** in the sense that he has been able to successfully transcend alleged childhood dyslexia, reading/learning disabilities, and the impact of both his parent's neurotic personality and character disorders on his identity and personality development. He is his own person, psychological warts and all.

I think many psychiatrists, psychologists, and psychoanalysts would feel bowled over and intimidated at a non-doctor patient interview by the aggressive, intuitive, and paradoxically charming Donald Trump. Or, for that matter, Lyndon Johnson in his political heyday. In fact, many psychiatrists seem to quickly mislabel Trump's actions and words as impulsive, impulse-ridden, lying, irrational, and even dangerous. They seem to regard Trump's actions and words as technical "**acting out**"[9] as if he were in psychotherapy. Acting out for many psychiatrists is thus tinged with a negative connotation.

Psychotherapist psychiatrists, psychologists, and psychoanalysts

---

[8] **Compensation** refers to the psychological defense mechanism by which a person overachievers in one area to compensate for failures in another. This psychological strategy allows people to disguise inadequacies, frustrations, stresses, or even neuropsychological problems by directing energy toward excelling or achieving in other areas.

[9] **Acting out:** Expression of unconscious emotional conflicts or feelings in actions rather than words. The person is not consciously aware of the meaning of such acts (American Psychiatric Association Glossary, 1994).

prefer their patients to use words to mentalize and reflect on a path to insight as a means to resolve conflict and mature as persons in psychotherapy. Trump uses words as actions and acts politically to back up and implement his words in executive action. His empathy and compassion are found in his relentless words of persuasion, provocation, and evocation of action in the form of legislation he can sign into law or as presidential orders. His political conversations are really a series of trial-and-error posturing on the way to a political action or compromise.

In a sense, we psychotherapists and psychoanalysts prefer "acting in" via verbalizing and mentalizing behavior in words at therapy sessions. Donald Trump matures, loves, and empathizes through actions and words as acts of honest political ambivalence, love, hate, and accomplishment.

Final Summary About the Misunderstood Mind of Donald Trump

A caveat and final generalization is that we all, of course, have personalities with degrees of neurotic personality traits (obsessive, compulsive, hysterical, paranoid, dependent, depressive, and hypomanic, etc.) that do not rise to the level of a clinical neurosis diagnosis. We may even have transient, neurotic, anxiety symptoms or conflicts that do not rise to the level of diagnosis or require treatment. In fact, contemporary psychiatrists do not use neurosis as psychoanalysts have traditionally used it for making a diagnosis. Some psychoanalysts are not very satisfied with the exclusion of neurosis as a diagnosis but accept the contemporary categories of various subdivided "anxiety disorders" used in diagnostic manuals.

In addition, and certainly important, is that psychiatrists, psychoanalysts, and psychologists are ethically committed to not making formal diagnostic statements about a public figure unless they have personally examined the person (the so-called Goldwater Rule). In our contemporary world however, journalists, pundits, academics, and educated people know enough about psychology that this domain becomes a conscious part of the social and political discourse. In this context, psychiatrists, psychoanalysts, and psychologists feel compelled, for many reasons, to voice our opinions as citizens and valued experts. But as FDR has been quoted as saying, "There are as many opinions as there are experts."

I repeat in conclusion, Donald Trump's personality, leadership style, and governance is a tangled skein of ego strength, resilience, and a successfully **compensated** pattern of phallic aggressive, hypomanic, and narcissistic personality traits. Trump uses defense mechanisms such as externalization, denial, and projection, which are regarded by many psychoanalysts as less healthy defenses. Such cerebrally oriented psychoanalysts would seem to prefer that Trump use intellectualization, sublimation, rationalization, and Kleinian depressive defensive positions. Trump is psychologically **compensated** in the sense that he has been able to successfully transcend alleged childhood dyslexia, reading/learning disabilities, and the impact of both his parents' neurotic personality patterns on his identity and personality.

The Obsession with Winning: The Cost and Tragic Flaw of Donald Trump's Compensations, or Maybe a Comeback American's Love?

Like all of us humans, Donald Trump has flaws, tragic flaws. During Trump's maturation and psychological development, the relentless drive to succeed and **be a winner**, as his father demanded and rewarded, led to deficits in Donald's capacity for empathy and nurturing of less aggressive and successful persons. Winning and working hard successfully gain Trump's respect and admiration. Trump's favored solutions for less fortunate people was primarily to provide jobs and work, hard work. Failures in an employee apprentice meant, "You're fired." Even initially beloved General "Mad Dog" Mattis suffered such fate from Trump … and perhaps for good reasons in the long run.

Other "Impaired" Politicians and Their Compensations

FDR was medically impaired with post-polio paraplegia. If George McGovern had not dropped Thomas Eagleton as his running mate because Eagleton had been successfully treated with ECT for depression and Eagleton had later run for president, it would have been an opportunity for Americans to accept successful compensation for mental illness in an effective political leader.

The COVID-19 pandemic frustrated and confounded Trump. It shattered Trump's vaunted friendship with President Xi. Trump felt betrayed and wounded. Trump's victories of huge job creation and a booming American economy were wounded by a tiny China virus. His energetic efforts focused on the Nobel Prize worthy efforts at Operation Warp Speed, which obtained a vaccine in world record time. Trump and Jared Kushner's Middle East peace plan (Abraham Accords) based on economic incentives and hard work was a creative foreign policy innovation. Trump's choice of Mike Pence with his steady presence to head up the daily efforts of the COVID response team was effective and provided persistent empathy. Inserting Trump's own aggressive presence during the daily meetings became a distraction and fake news battles with the hostile liberal press. Trump's own poor tolerance for losing and ad hominem attacks on political opponents during his campaign and his governing, became and are still self-defeating as well as still being used against him.

The Trump Rally on January 6th, 2021, Perturbed My Mind About Trump Again!

It will take a long time for the facts to emerge about what happened at the US Capital on January 6th, 2021. It does seem clear to me that Trump's tragic flaw of an intense obsession with winning and not being a loser was prominent that day. I think he underestimated the power of his charisma on some violent disturbed followers who had long before January 6th planned violence that began before Trump finished his powerful speech. Trump did not want physical violence in any form! I do not feel he encouraged violence at the capital. Just the opposite. He urged peaceful, appropriate demonstrations he saw as a strong political form of fighting. Trump's expressed disdain for Vice President Pence if he did not do as Trump wished was another reflection of Trump's tragic flaw obsession with not being a loser! Win at all costs. Trump's negative comments about Pence may have led to danger for Mike Pence.

Tragically, in fact, the January 6th violence prevented the last chance for effective legitimate presentation of the cases of unconstitutional election practices in Pennsylvania, Michigan, Wisconsin, Arizona, and Georgia to the Congress that, if accepted, could have changed the electoral count officiated by Vice President Pence at the Capital.

In addition, Trump's obsession about being a loser of the presidential election clouded and negatively affected the Senate elections in Georgia. It seemed to cause many Trump supporters in Georgia to be discouraged about voting because of Trump's emphasis on his own having been cheated of a victory. Trump instead should have focused on the importance of defeating the Democrat Senate candidates.

Trump's recent speech at CPAC clearly expresses Trump's political call to political battle that continues with a fury, within him, and from him as Trump is perceived as losing the election. The ultimate fear and failure of being the loser! Perhaps a comeback that Americans love?

Final Thoughts About Donald Trump and January 6th

The jolting events of January 6th, 2021, were an American populist political tragedy/comedy of errors, and a reflection of Donald Trump's tragic flaw and psychological blind spot.

The Tragedy/Comedy of Errors on January 6th, 2021

Formal objections to certification of presidential election votes in congress as the vice president presides has occurred many times in American history, including when Al Gore presided and the vote count to defeat him was certified against many objections by Democrat congresspersons. In essence Hillary Clinton has not stopped protesting her defeat for all four years of Donald Trump's falsely maligned presidency. Clinton still will not accept her defeat to this day!

Unfortunately, Donald Trump lost his composure and much of his credibility with many Americans when he hyperbolically and exaggeratingly trumpeted over simplified cries of widespread election fraud as if it was legally proven fact. Trump and his legal advisers made too scattered and not fully investigated or fully proven claims about voting machine error, inappropriately harvested mailed in ballots, ballot-counting cheating, and unconstitutional actions by state legislatures in Pennsylvania, Michigan, Arizona,

Wisconsin, and Georgia. Trump continued his stollen election theme during the ill-fated senatorial elections in Georgia, which was a factor in Republicans losing the Georgia Senate elections and control of the Senate! Trump continues this pied piper hyperbole music to this day. Trump has been personally and politically obsessed with winning at all costs and **never, ever, being a loser**. Sometimes a humble loser who learns from the experience becomes the real winner.

Despite Trump's tragic and rigid position, there actually were serious constitutional violations by the battleground state legislatures that were not thoroughly heard by the Supreme Court as Justices Alito and Thomas have stated clearly. There was not enough time for all the full investigations to be made that would have perhaps convinced SCOTUS to consider the violations sufficient to change the outcome of the 2020 presidential election. Trump and his lawyers were never granted a full hearing by SCOTUS. Election fraud investigations even before COVID-19 days take a long time and proving election fraud legally, with subsequent legal consequences, takes a long time and much election fraud is never or rarely detected or proven.

It is also clear that the COVID-19 pandemic and the resulting massive use of mailed in ballots made the 2020 election controversial as well as fraught with questionable tactics by both political parties as Mollie Hemingway describes in her book, *Rigged: How the Media, Big Tech, and the Democrats Seized Our Elections*, and Molly Ball in her detailed *Time* magazine article, "The Secret History of the Shadow Campaign That Saved the 2020 Election." Ball, from a liberal Democrat point of view, and Hemingway, from a conservative Republican point of view, both locate the dangerous domains of American political election tampering and mischief.

The dark tragic comedy of January 6th also did not allow the full and careful presentation by conservative Republicans of integrity like Ted Cruz, Jim Jordan, and Louie Gohmert of the constitutional violations of the battleground states to Mike Pence and both houses of Congress where the election votes may have been appropriately challenged and possibly changed. Trump should have been more in touch with the large group impact of his charisma on a few of his destructive followers who committed crimes at the capital. Trump did insist his followers peacefully demonstrate but he did not or could not lead the group of protestors or send a plenipotentiary (a cabinet member like Ben Carson or even his son) to lead the protest effectively and peacefully at the Capitol. A definitively peaceful protest on January 6th, 2021, might have changed the course of American history. The constitution clearly specifies that the certification of the vote count by Congress is not merely a ceremonial or mechanical perfunctory process.

Donald Trump's Tragic Flaw and Psychological Blind Spot Punctuated on January 6th

Donald Trump's personality, leadership style, and governance is a tangled skein of ego strength, resilience, and a successfully **compensated** pattern of phallic aggressive, hypomanic, and narcissistic personality traits. Trump uses defense mechanisms such as externalization, denial, and projection, which are regarded by many psychoanalysts as less healthy defenses. Such cerebrally oriented psychoanalysts would seem to prefer that Trump use intellectualization, sublimation, rationalization, and Kleinian depressive defensive positions. Trump is psychologically **compensated** in the sense that he has been able to successfully transcend his childhood dyslexia, reading/learning disabilities, and the impact of both his parent's neurotic personality and character traits on his identity, personality, and destiny.

Like all of us humans, Donald Trump has flaws, tragic flaws. **The tragic flaw of Donald Trump's personality is an obsession with winning.** His mantra is "never be a loser!" During Trump's maturation and psychological development, the relentless drive to succeed and **be a winner** as his father demanded and rewarded, led to deficits in Donald's capacity for empathy and nurturing of less aggressive and successful persons. Winning and working hard successfully gain Trump's respect and admiration. Trump's favored solutions for less fortunate people was primarily to provide jobs and work, hard work. Failures in an employee apprentice meant, "you're fired". Even the initially beloved General "Mad Dog" Mattis suffered such fate from Trump as did Tillerson, Sessions, and even Mike Pence perhaps one of our very best vice presidents.

A profound truth eludes Donald Trump, sometimes a loser that learns from the experience of losing becomes a winner. Trump a lover of sports, should know that even if a team gets bad calls from the umpires, even if opponents cheat, even if they lose, they can learn from a defeat.

A corollary to Trump's tragic flaw is his unfortunate propensity to insult his political opponents flagrantly and crudely, even members of his own political party. He insulted Carly Fiorina's face during the primary race before his election as president. This practice seems to be used in order for Trump to be a winner at all costs—but at any costs is dangerous. An illustration of this is found in reporting in *The Wall Street Journal* on October 2, 2022, where Trump's tirade against Mitch McConnell is described. Trump alleged that McConnell approved trillions of dollars of Democrat bills without negotiation because he hates Trump and "knows I am strongly opposed to them, or is he doing it because he believes in the Fake and Highly Destructive Green New Deal, and is willing to take the Country down with him?"

Trump then wrote on Truth Social, saying that McConnell had a "DEATH WISH" and, "should seek help and advice from his China loving wife, Coco Chow!"

The Wall Street Journal article reports further:

> This continues Mr. Trump's attacks on Elaine Chao, Mr.
> McConnell's wife, for being Chinese American. Her real

offense was resigning as transportation secretary after Mr. Trump's disgraceful behavior on Jan. 6. His feud with Mr. McConnell is also personal, as the Kentucky Senator condemned Mr. Trump's Jan. 6 actions and (McConnell), hasn't spoken to him since. The "death wish" rhetoric is ugly even by Mr. Trump's standards and deserves to be condemned (WSJ, October 2, 2022).

In fact, unhinged supporters of Trump could misconstrue his bellicose hyperbole about McConnell, Mike Pence, and others and take unfortunate murderous action that Trump would never intend. He needs to stay strong in his political message but avoid truly dangerous carelessly stated hyperbole.

Regardless, an anti-Trump phenomenon is rampant and real in America. Trump contributes to this phenomenon and seems to enjoy the ad hominem theater despite its self-defeating results. His loyal followers love him for his flaws or despite them.

Trump is a man of action, not words. Words are mere vehicles toward political action as political promise-keeping. Trump uses words as actions and acts politically to back up and implement his words in executive action. His empathy and compassion are in his relentless words of persuasion, provocation, and evocation of action in the form of legislation he can sign into law or as presidential orders. Trump's political conversations are really a series of trial-and-error posturing on the way toward a political action or compromise. Perhaps a comeback that Americans love will happen for Trump in 2024. Sadly, I don't support Trump in 2024 unless Biden/Harris run again or Democrat candidates of their political ilk emerge.

In my over fifty years in medicine, psychiatry, and psychoanalysis, some of my most valued discoveries have been the experience of observing people for whom the textbooks would predict pain or disaster, but who triumphed over adversity to live unusually successful lives. I think Donald Trump, a flawed but effective person, is one of them. It is sad how his tragic flaw and blind spot dominated the final events of the 2020 election and his administration.

Trump certainly should or could be remembered for his "Operation Warp Speed" that allowed a record-breaking speed in producing a Covid-19 vaccine; the Nobel Peace Prize deserving "Abraham Accords" that started genuine paths to peace in the Middle East based on economic progress and cooperation as opposed to endless ideologic negotiations; a vigorous pre-Covid-19 low inflation economy with energy independence progress; and finally, restraining little rocket man Kim's aggressive behavior through mano-a-mano, face-to-face talk. Perhaps an American comeback may occur for Trump in the 2024 presidential election.

Appendix

Trump the Political Aggressor, Identification with the Aggressor*, and Hatred of the Aggressor by the Group Self*
*The phrase "**identification with the aggressor**" was coined by Sandor Ferenczi. It is a paradoxical behavior that can only be explained as a defense mechanism, which involves the victim of aggression or harm acting like the **aggressor**. Dec 17, 2016

https://exploringyourmind.com/identification-with-the-aggressor/

***Group self:** There is a parallel process by which an individual's sense of himself as part of a group is formed. In essence, inner representations of our self and our self-in-a-group are parallel and conjoined during early developmental and maturational personality experiences. In 1976, Heinz Kohut described **the group self**. (*The Search for the Self: Selected Writings of Heinz Kohut,* 1950-1978, Volume 2, Paul Ornstein, ed. Footnote #21, pp 837-838 and in destructive cult leaders in *Malignant Pied Pipers* by Peter Olsson, 2017, p.164-165.)

In individual psychology, psychoanalysts describe **identification with the aggressor** in their work with individuals, particularly traumatized individuals. In observing Trump operate politically, it is striking to observe what can be called **identification with and or, hatred of the aggressor** at the large group psychological level. In his large political rallies, Trump is applauded, cheered, and adored by the crowds of supporters as he insults, demeans, and caricatures political opponents. They radiate an almost joyful identification with their aggressor hero, Donald Trump. Many in Trump's campaign style crowds have felt traumatized and hurt by trade and other government policies that they feel took their jobs away in the oil, coal, or manufacturing industries. Trump was their aggressor savior.

Democrat, and even some Republican politicians, however, more than resent and hate Trump at subconscious and conscious levels because of his aggressive, bullying, political style and behavior. They seem to feel victimized or traumatized emotionally and politically. Trump sometimes starts such political fights, and certainly, if attacked, will predictably escalate his aggression to win a personal fight at all costs.

Review Requested:
We'd like to know if you enjoyed the book. Please consider leaving a review on the platform from which you purchased the book.